today's culture facilities

Edition 2006

Author: Eduard Broto
Graphic designer & production: Pilar Chueca
Text: contributed by the architects, edited by William George

© Carles Broto i Comerma
Jonqueres, 10, 1-5
08003 Barcelona, Spain
Tel.: +34 93 301 21 99
 Fax: +34-93-301 00 21
E-mail: info@linksbooks.net
www. linksbooks.net

today's culture facilities

index

today's **culture** facilities

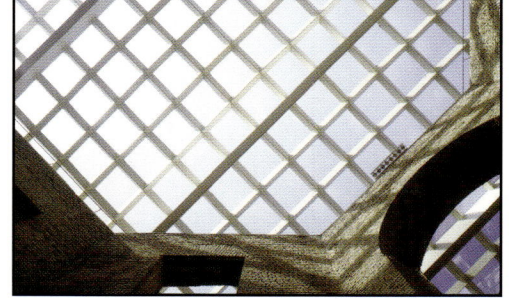

INTRODUCTION

If there is a discipline in which human development is absolutely clear, it is architecture. By considering the evolution of forms of construction through the ages, any observer could trace the long and irregular path taken by historical development; the techniques of design, technological innovations, the evolution of trends and the formation of schools inevitably reflect the character, the "soul" of each civilization. At the present time we find a wide range of schools that coexist and are interrelated: Rationalism, the Modern Movement, technology an aesthetic form, Postmodernism, the return to classical orders, the recovery of local forms and building materials, Deconstructivism and ecological architecture.

Where is the true spirit of innovation? Who are the true creators of our time? What orders, what trends, are recognized as the most representative of the late 20th century? Answering these questions is no easy task, and cannot be done in this monographic volume devoted to projects related to culture. Our aim is merely to offer an honest, and we hope balanced, panorama of some projects that in our opinion can be considered as worthy representatives of the building fashions of our generation.

Indeed, in order to present representative works of the architecture of recent years we avoided a preference for any tendency, basing our selection solely on aesthetic criteria and the outstanding interest of the projects.

Mario Botta
Museum of Modern Art

San Francisco, USA

Located on Third Street, near the Moscone Convention Center, the museum, which opened on January 18, 1995, is part of an urban redevelopment programme covering an area of more than 40 hectares. With this building, Mario Botta, who has joined the elite group of international architects who determine predominant styles, shows once more through the modernity of his geometry that his architecture retains a kind of primordial strength which sets it apart from any movement. The building is located across the street from Fumihiko Maki´s new Yerba Buena Center, whose light seems at odds with Botta´s brick veneer cladding and massive, almost windowless design.
A central oculus which appears on the exterior of the building in the form of a truncated cylinder brings light to the five stories of the building, and particularly to the generous, 7-metre high top-lit galleries on the upper floor.

Photographs: Richard Barnes

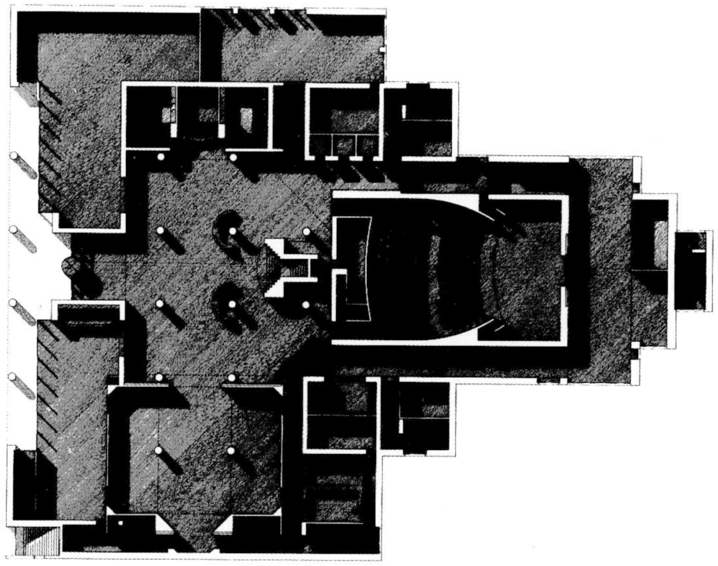

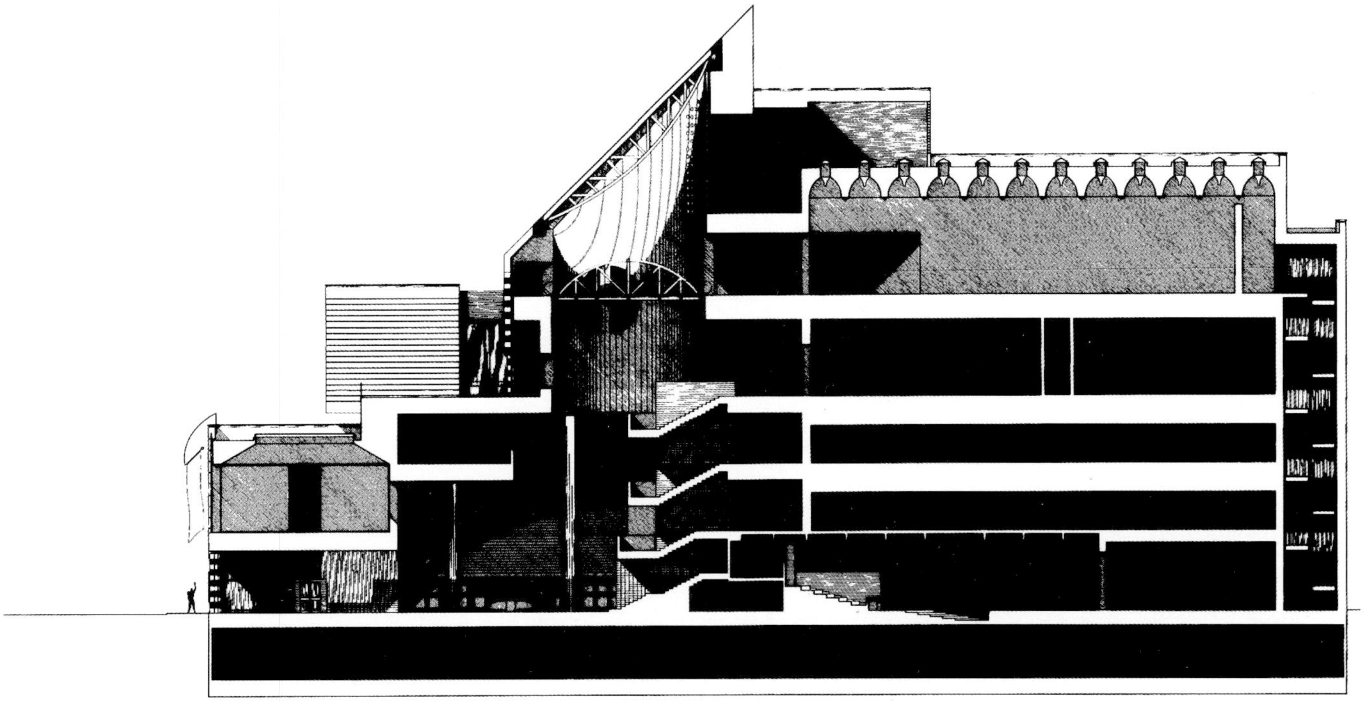

The exhibition hall located on the upper floor is accessed by means of a bridge that spans the gap left by the central oculus.

Frank O. Gehry & Associates
Museum Guggenheim Bilbao

Bilbao, Spain

Designed by the architect Frank O. Gehry, the Guggenheim Museum in Bilbao is located on a plot of 32,500 sqm at the same level as the Nervión estuary, i.e. 16 m below the level of the city, bounded at one end by the Puente de la Salve, one of the main entrances to the city.

The building is composed of a series of interconnected volumes, some orthogonal and clad in limestone, and others curved and twisting, with a titanium skin. These volumes are combined with glazed curtain walls that give the museum great transparency. The main entrance is on one of the main streets that cross Bilbao diagonally, in an attempt to extend the urban centre right to the door of the museum. A large flight of steps leads down into the foyer, thus solving the difference in height between the estuary and the expansion area of the city. Thus, this building with a floor area of 24,000 sqm and a height of over 50 m does not exceed the height of the surrounding buildings.

After crossing the foyer and entering the exhibition space, one reaches the atrium, one of the most characteristic features of the museum, crowned by a skylight in the form of a "metal flower", which floods the space with light. The terrace, which is accessed from the atrium and has views of the estuary and the water garden, is covered by a canopy supported on a single stone pillar, with a dual function of protection and aesthetics. A large flight of stairs goes up from the rear facade to the sculptural tower, which was designed to absorb and integrate the Puente de la Salve into the architectural complex.

The three levels of galleries are organised around this atrium and are connected by curvilinear walkways, glazed lifts and stair towers. As in a metaphorical city, where the panels of glass that cover the lift-well evoke the scales of a fish that leaps and spins, the walkways that climb the interior walls are like vertical motorways, and the plaster curves crowning the atrium suggest the moulded ribbing of a drawing by William de Kooning. In short, a glimpse of artifice in architectural design taken to its uttermost limits.

Photographs: Erika Barahona Ede

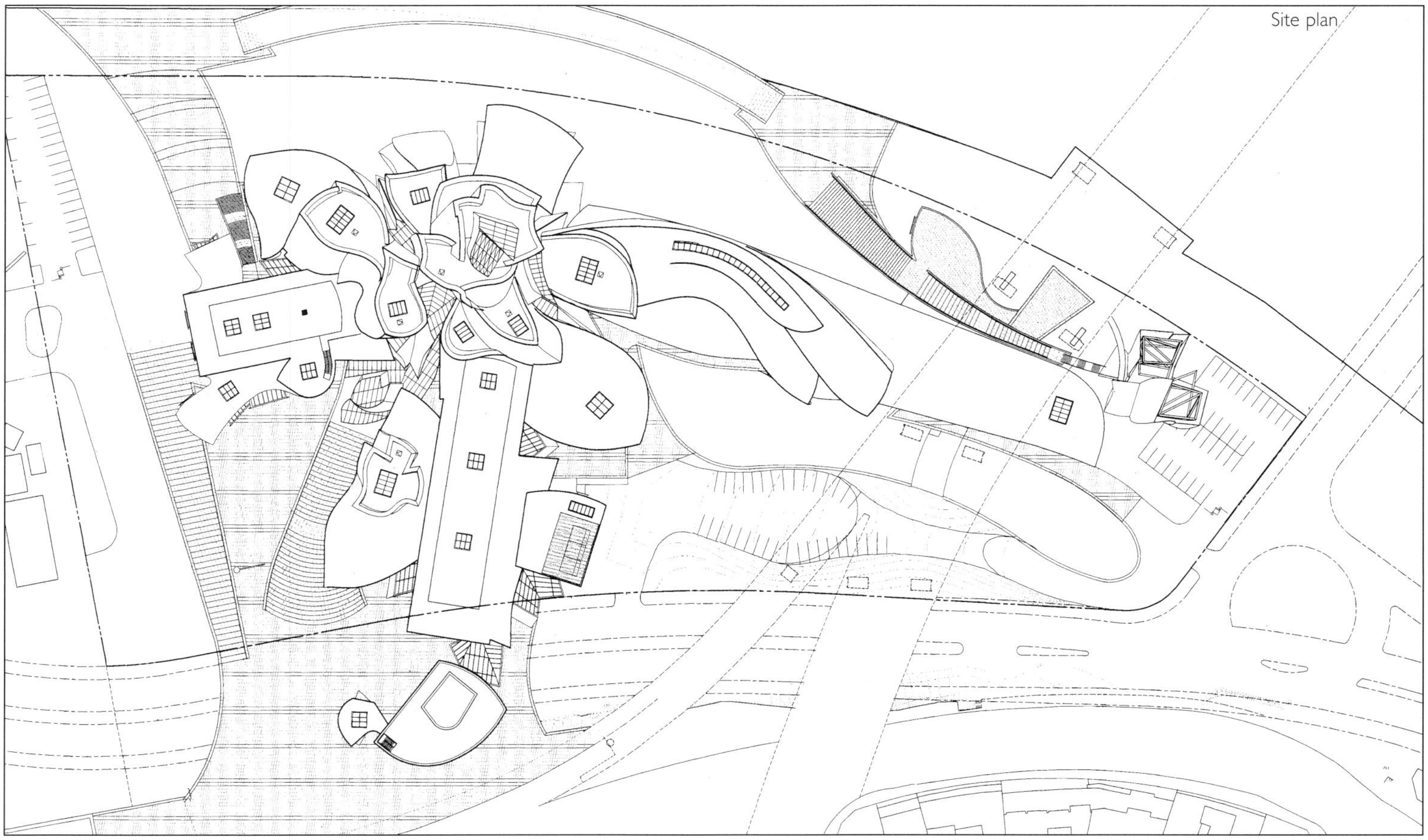

Site plan

South elevation

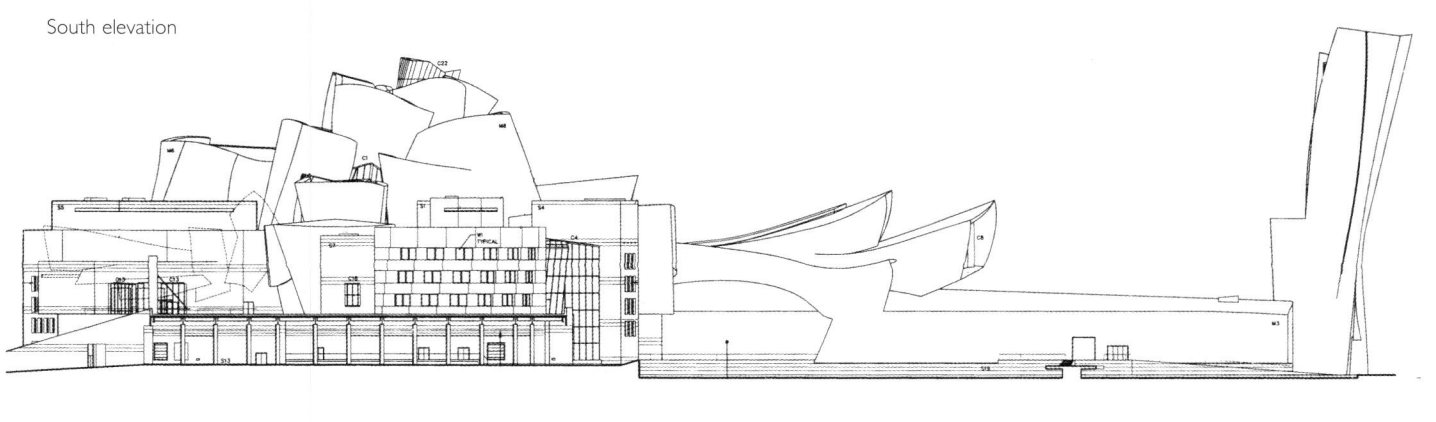

North elevation

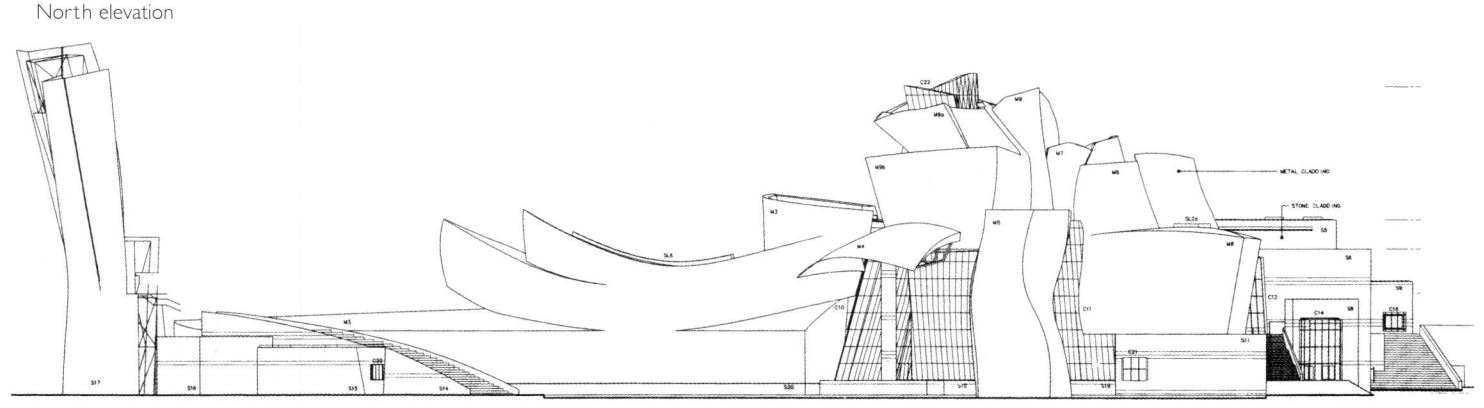

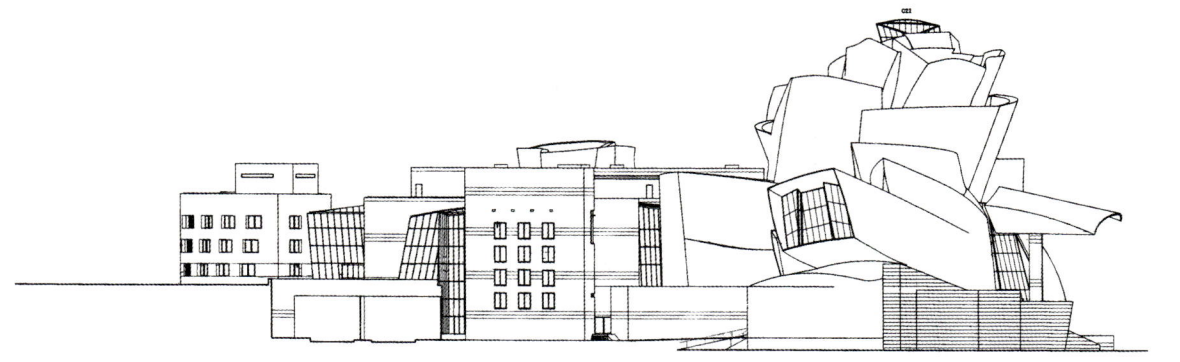

East elevation

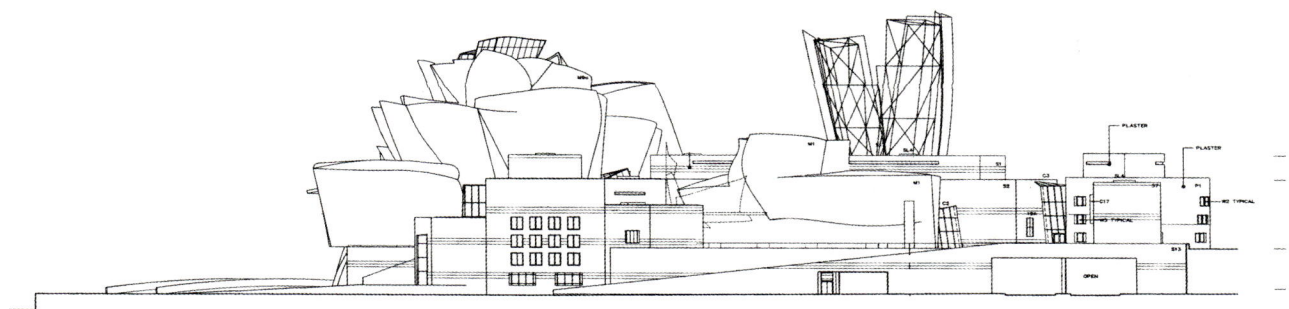

West elevation

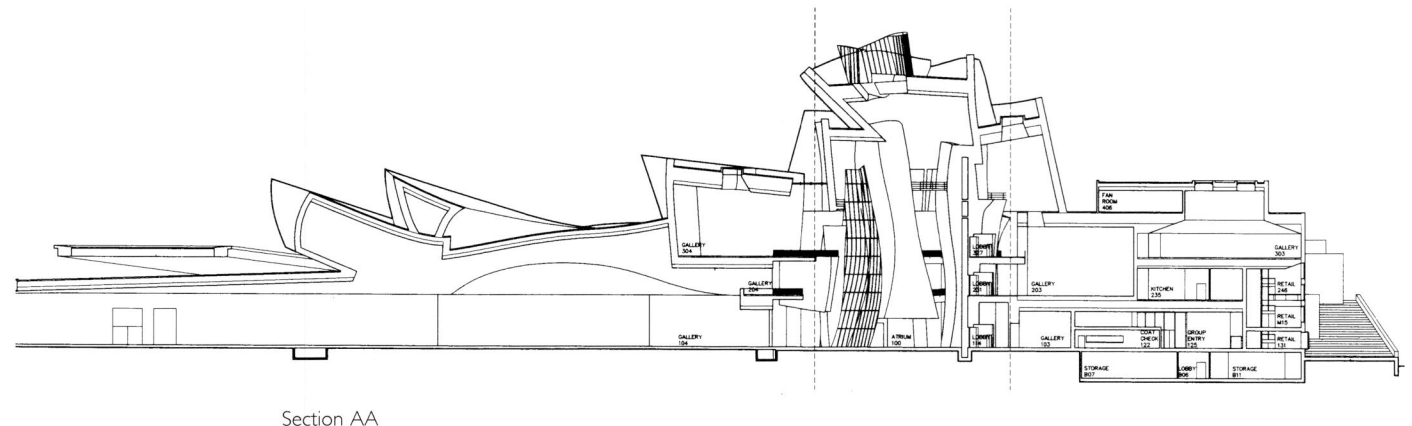

Section AA

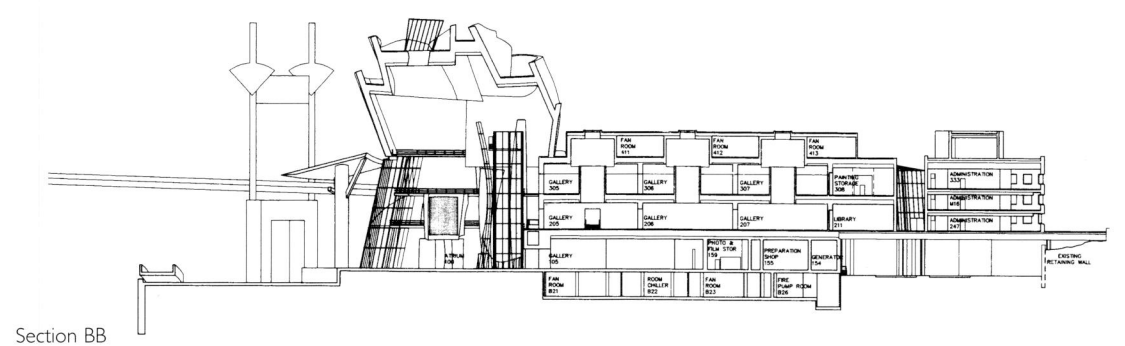

Section BB

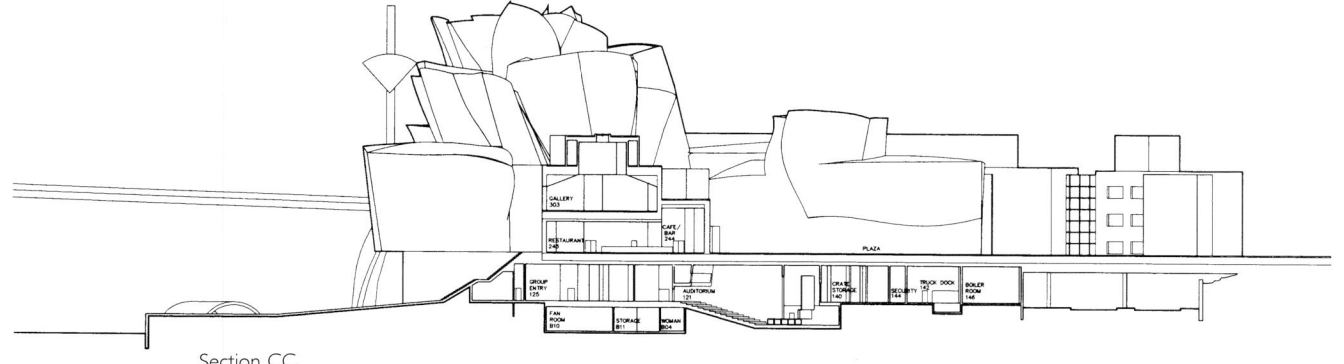

Section CC

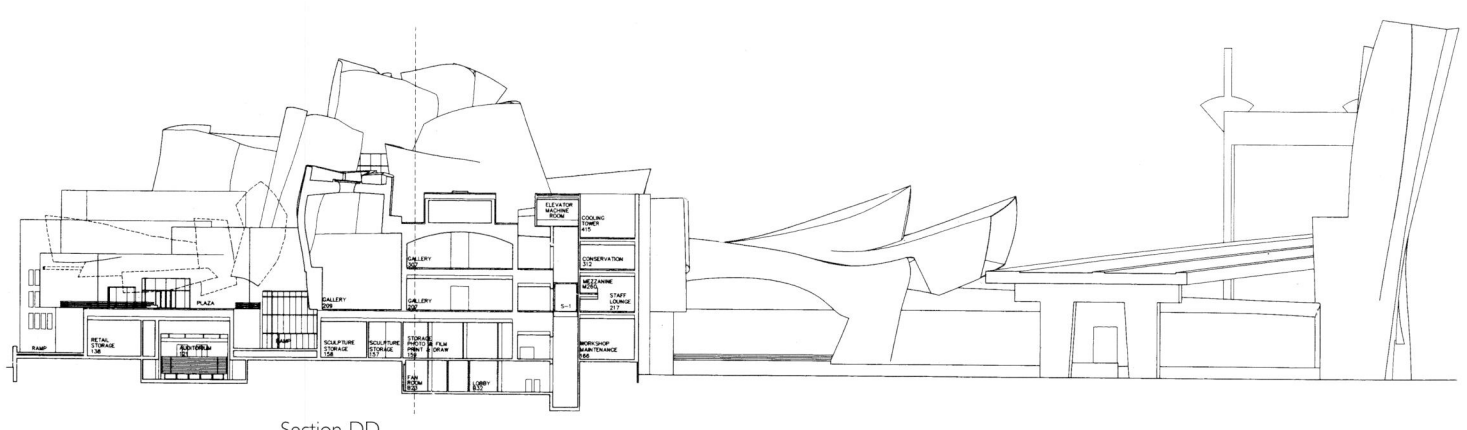

Section DD

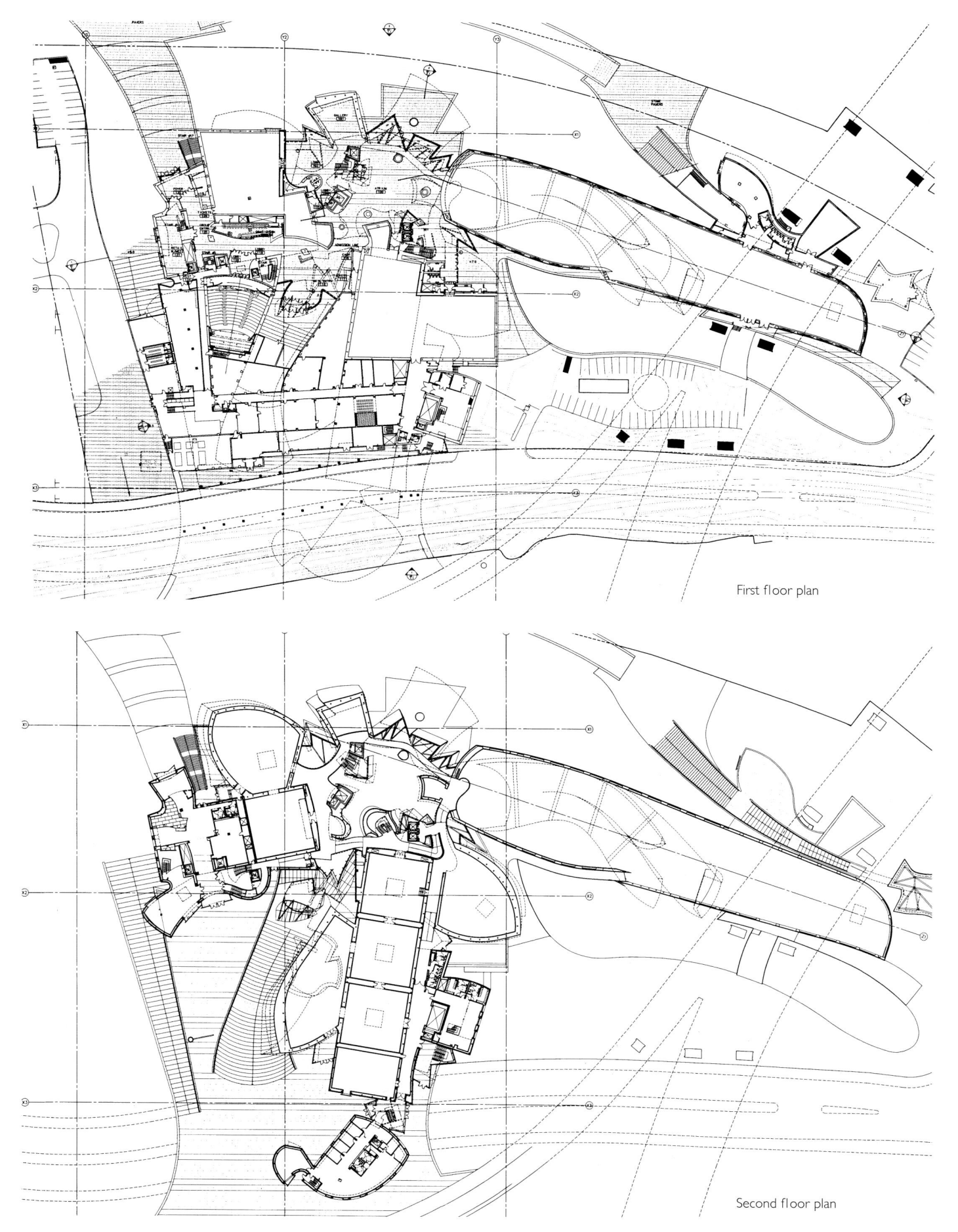

First floor plan

Second floor plan

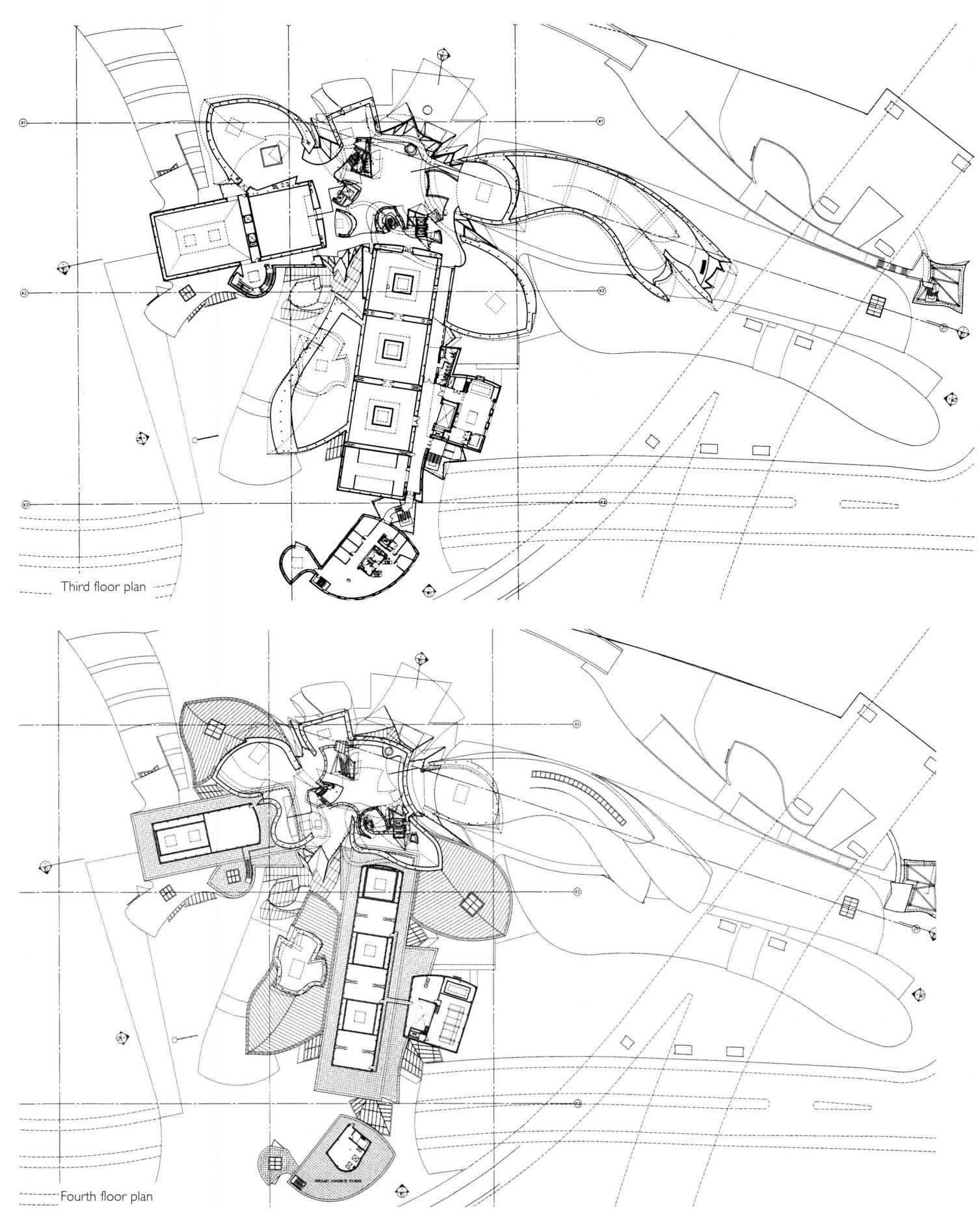

Third floor plan

Fourth floor plan

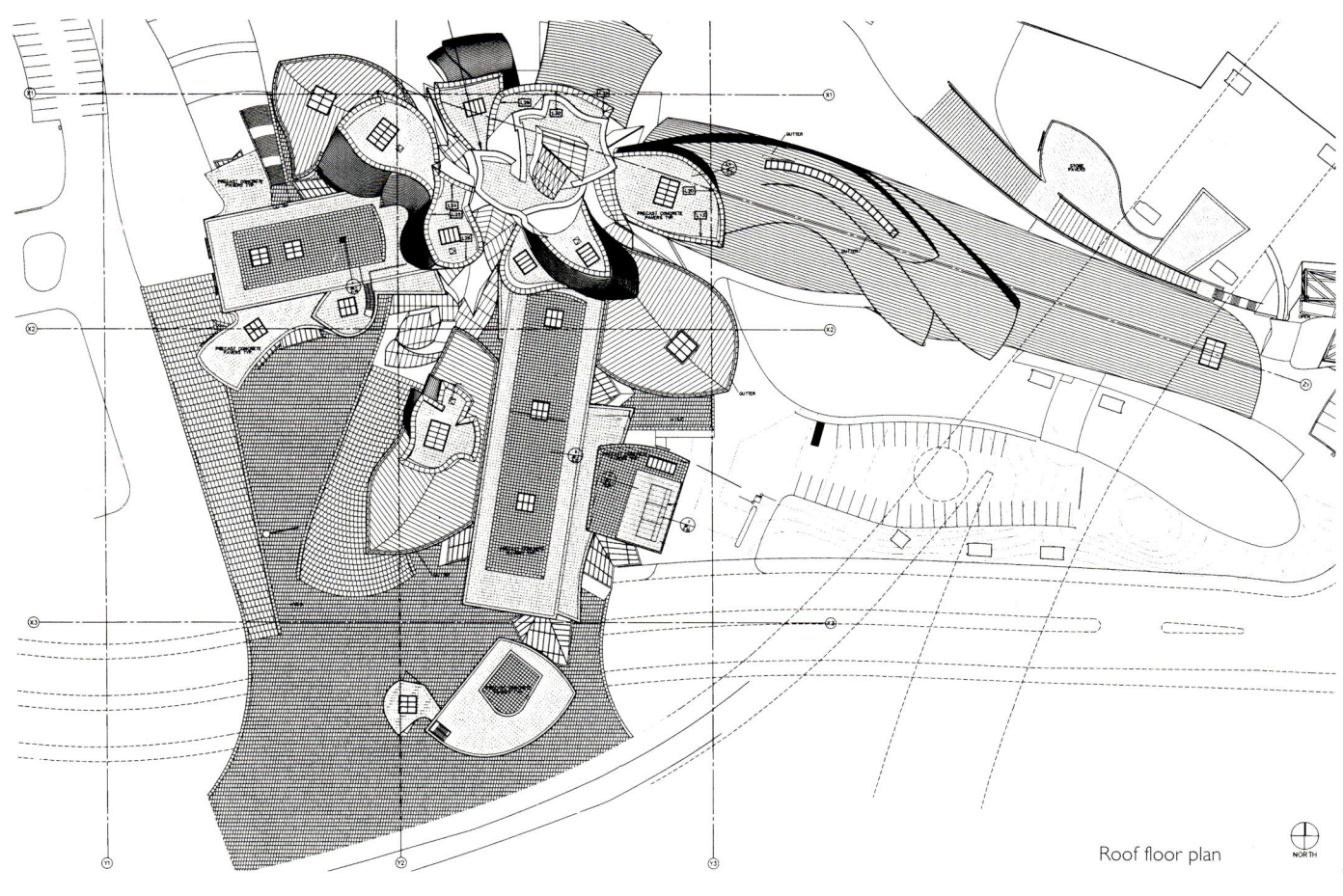

Roof floor plan

The building has a total of 11,000 sqm of exhibition space divided into nineteen galleries. Ten of them have an orthogonal shape, and can be identified from the exterior by their stone cladding. In contrast, the other nine halls are highly irregular and are identified from the exterior by their titanium cladding.

Shin Takamatsu & Associates
Shoji Ueda Museum of Photography

Tottori, Japan

This museum building consists of 4 concrete blocks (exhibition rooms) and 4 ponds. Each of the small ponds between the blocks reflects Mt. Daisen, which rises far behind the site.

Takamatsu´s design is in the mainstream of the latest in Japanese architecture, projecting a compact, restrained image, almost devoid of openings in the exterior walls and without aesthetic concessions of any kind.

This aesthetic approach exerts two distinct effects: it produces a slightly magical feeling of the veiled, the hidden, and a the same time it causes the view to be shifted towards the interior; the surroundings strike up a relationship with the built volume.

The visitor will encounter this beautiful scenery on moving from one exhibition hall to another, thereby enjoying and experiencing the surrounding nature.

There are two ways to relate nature and architecture: one is done by harmonizing them, and another is done by taking scenery into the architecture. In this museum, obviously the latter is adopted.

The scenery is experienced in a direct way. The museum is wrapped in concrete. By using concrete for the exterior, the museum seems to rise up from the ground. The curved concrete wall expresses the scale of Mt. Daisen.

A composition with small blocks provides a village-like image. That is, an active and at the same time a passive way of communicating with the scenery.

If architecture were words, the city would tell a story. Takamatsu´s architecture is a word with strong meaning.

Photographs: Nacása and Partners

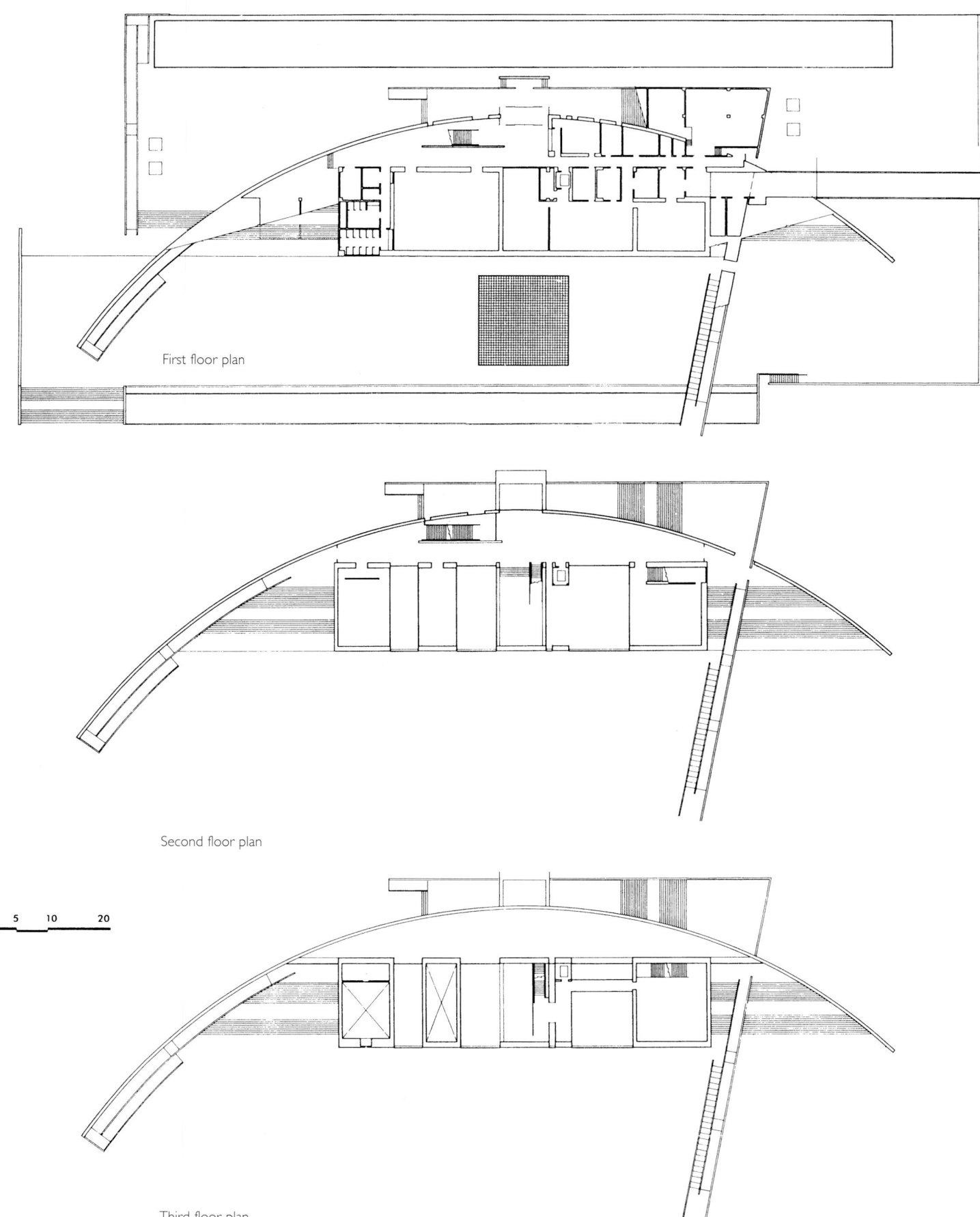

First floor plan

Second floor plan

0 5 10   20

Third floor plan

26

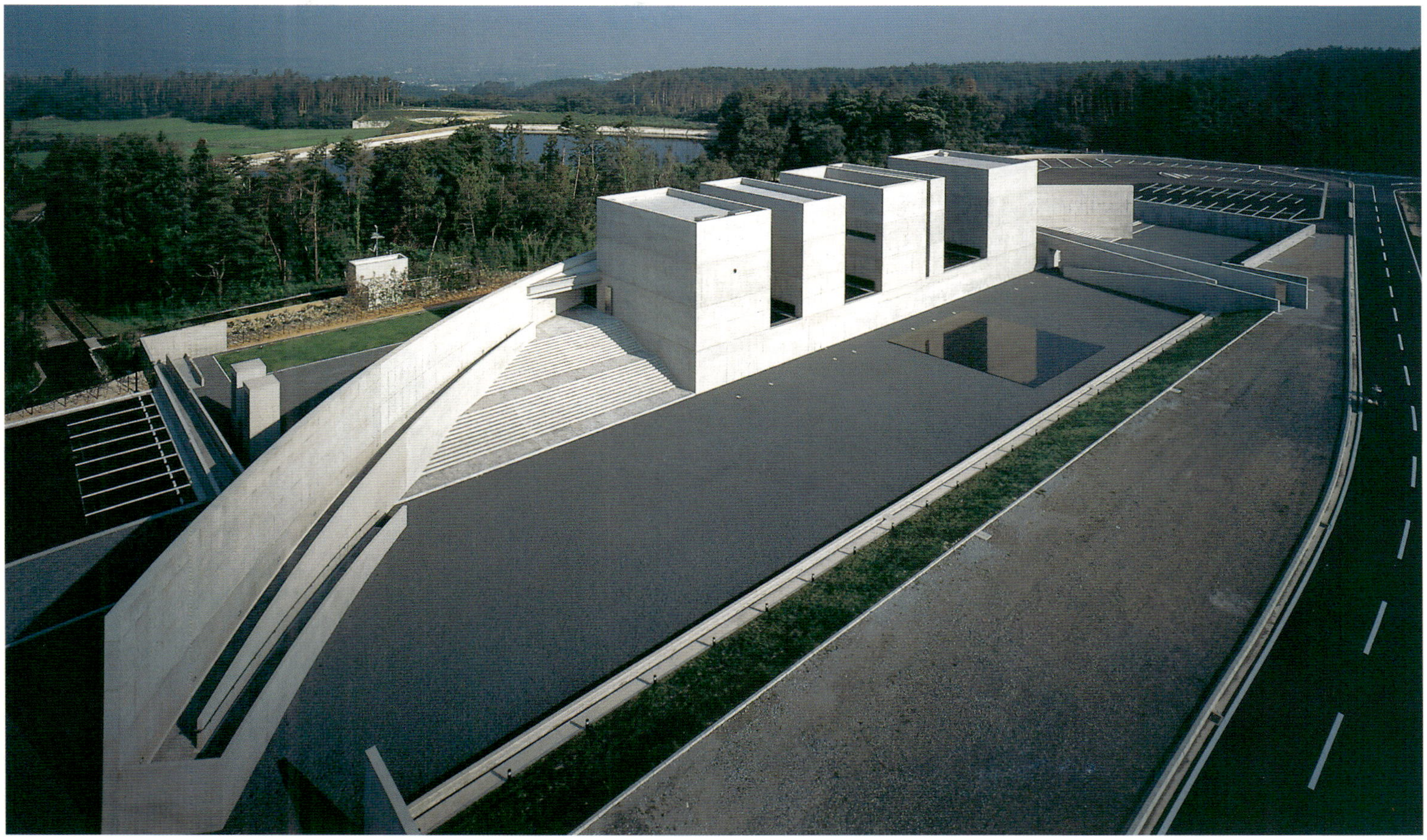

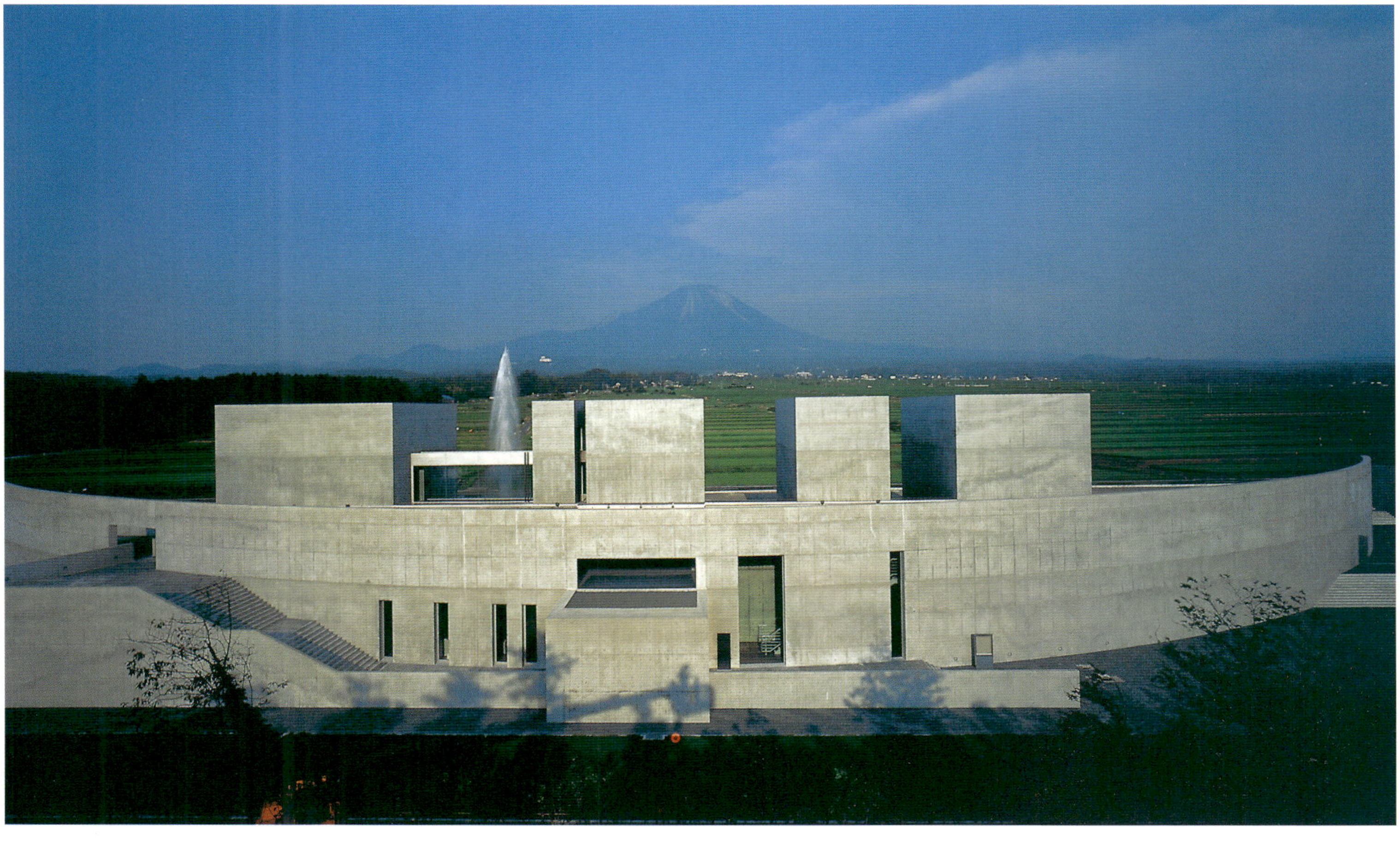

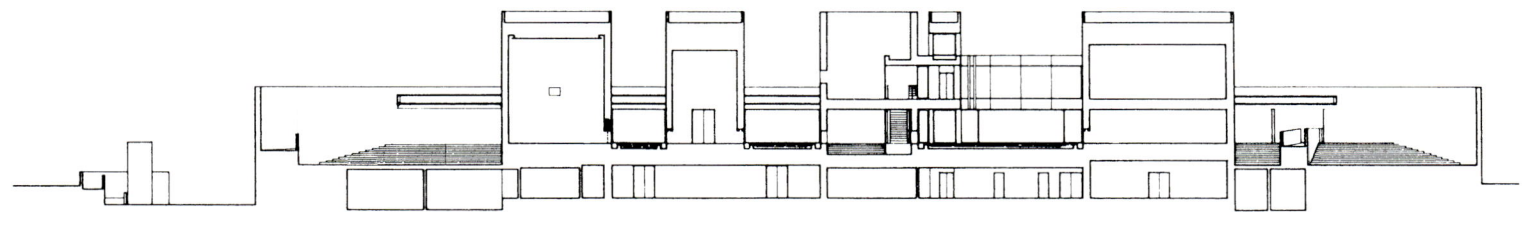

Longitudinal section

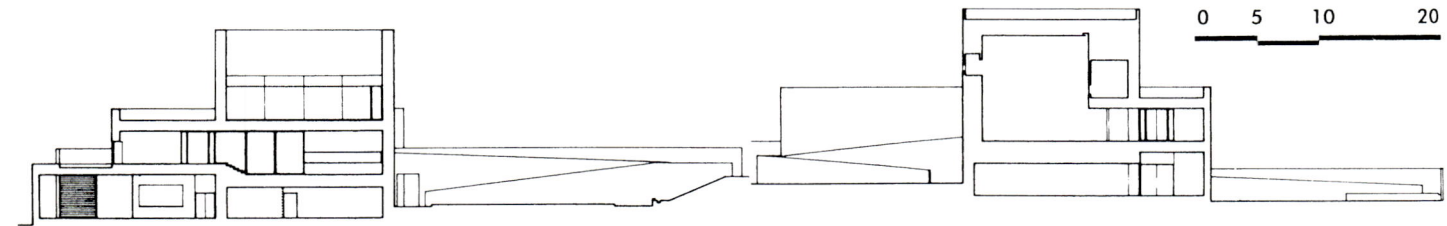

| 0 | 5 | 10 | | 20 |

Cross-sections

Takenaka's proposal is based on the abstraction and purity of the volumes and the use of clean materials: the four concrete blocks gain form a very forceful profile.

Each of the small ponds between the blocks reflects Mt. Daisen, which rises far behind the site. Visitors will encounter this beatiful scenery when they move from one enhibition hall to another.

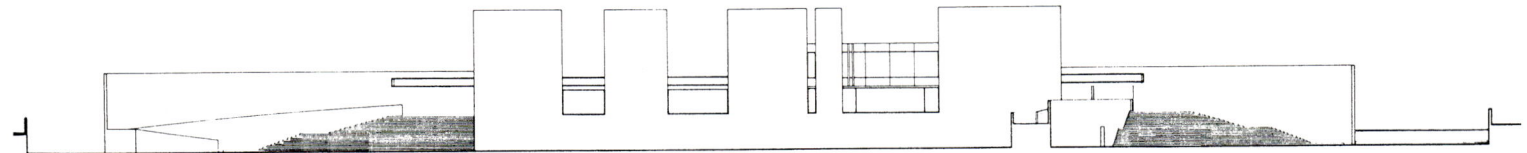

South-east elevation

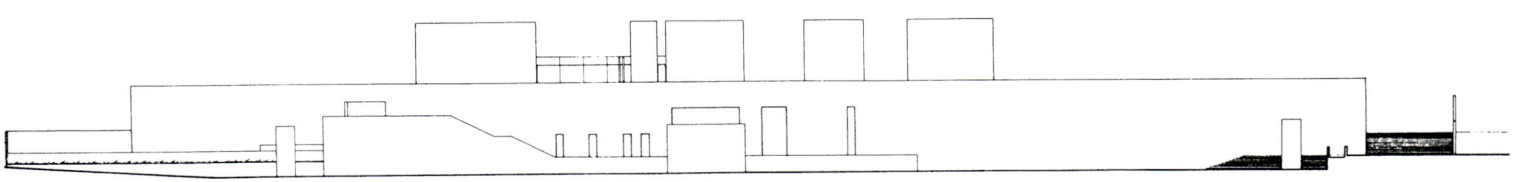

North-west elevation

Álvaro Siza
Contemporary Galician Art Centre

Santiago de Compostela, Spain

The building is located in an interesting and complex monumental area, on the edge of the historic centre of Santiago de Compostela on a new major thoroughfare, Rua de Ramón del Valle Inclán. The complex consists of a museum, a conference hall, art laboratories and exhibition rooms. A direct relation is established with the new part of the convent of Santo Domingo de Bonaval and the current museum of Galician Art, of which it seems to be a prolongation.

Siza presents the blind facade of the Centre as a high granite wall marking the limit of the property belonging to the convent, thus closing the corner giving onto Calle de Cara Molina. The front of the new building clearly closes the space created by the two main elements of the ecclesiastical complex (the church and the cloister), thus creating a small square containing the main accesses to the Centre.

A rotation of 21 degrees is established between the facade facing the main street and the cemetery behind the convent. This is coherent with the topographic structure and is taken as one of the organizing elements of the complex. Two large blocks are obtained from it: a compact block formed by the museum and its store-rooms, which belongs mainly to the structure of the garden; and a block containing an auditorium and a library which are oriented towards the street. The triangular space created between the two blocks is the main point of circulation.

The building has two floors plus a basement. It is organized around a central corridor that separates the museum from the services, and a terrace conceived as a sculpture garden that opens onto the urban landscape.

The outer cladding of granite panels, contrasting with the white plaster-work and marble used on the interior, favours the integration of the building in the monumental and ecclesiastic dimension of the city of Santiago.

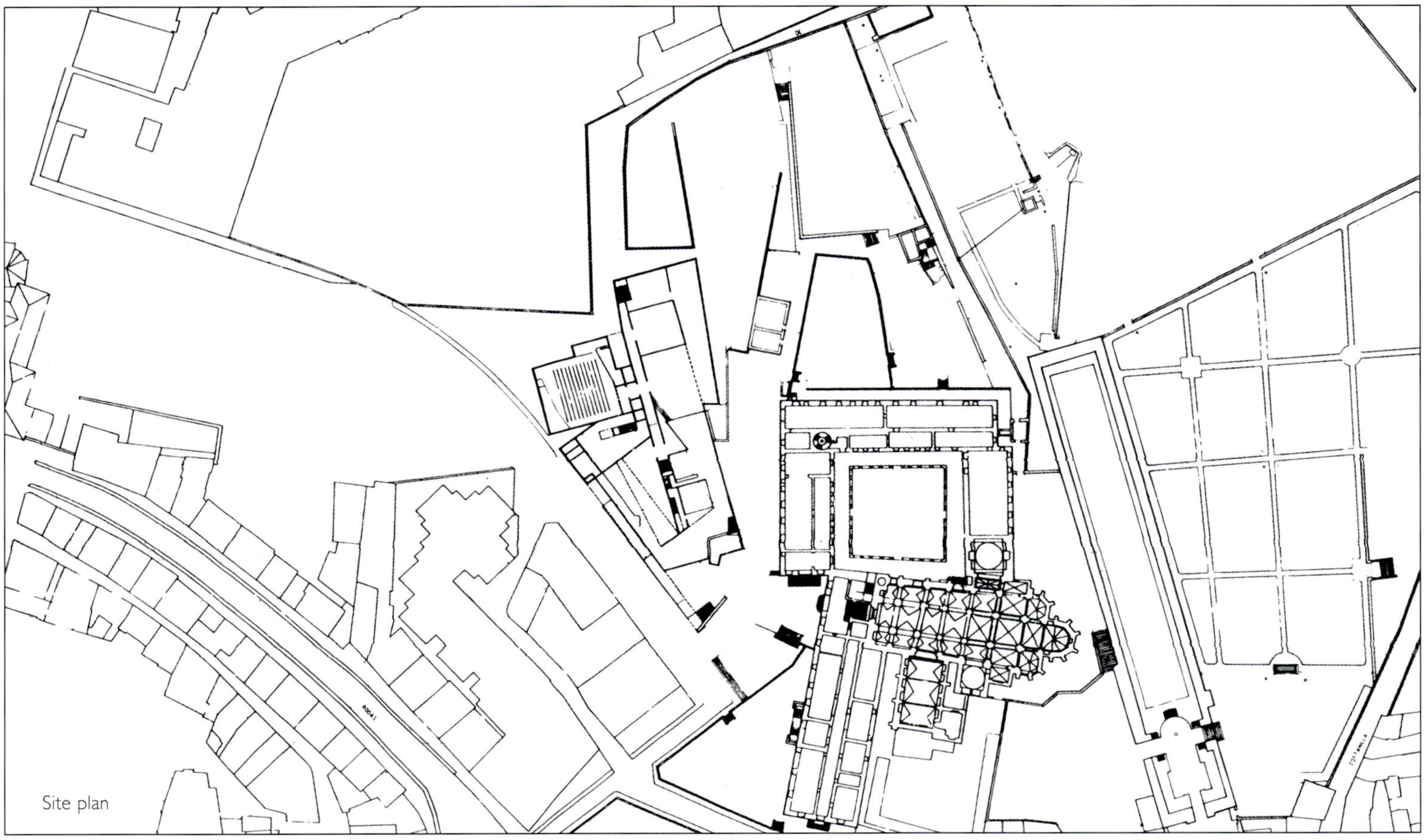

Site plan

The building is sited in one of the most interesting but complex zones at the edge of the historic city centre.

The front of the new building clearly encloses the space between the church and the cloister, thus creating a square with the main accesses to the new centre.

The outer cladding of granite panels contrasts with the whiteness of the plaster-work and marble used on the interior.

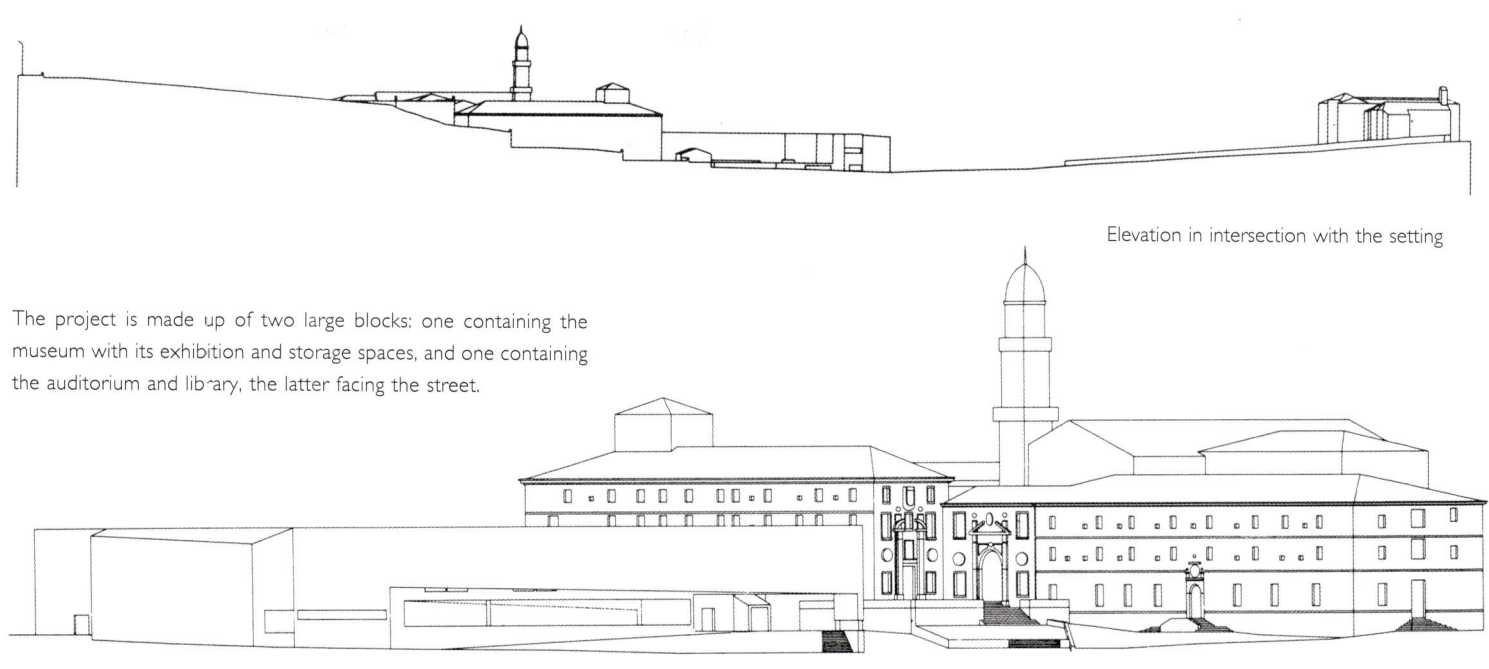

Elevation in intersection with the setting

The project is made up of two large blocks: one containing the museum with its exhibition and storage spaces, and one containing the auditorium and library, the latter facing the street.

North-east elevation

The museum building has two floors plus a basement, which are organized around a central corridor that also gives access to a terrace conceived as a garden of sculptures that is open to the exterior.

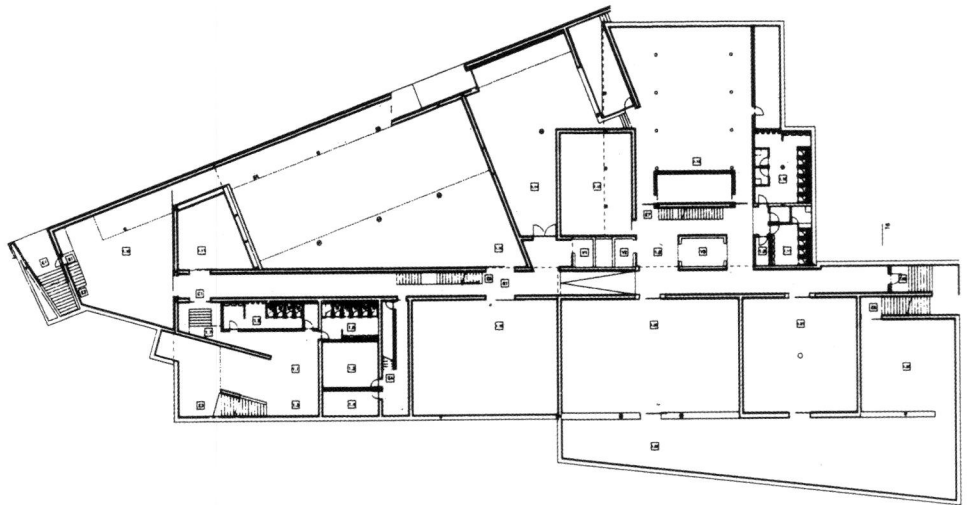

Basement floor plan

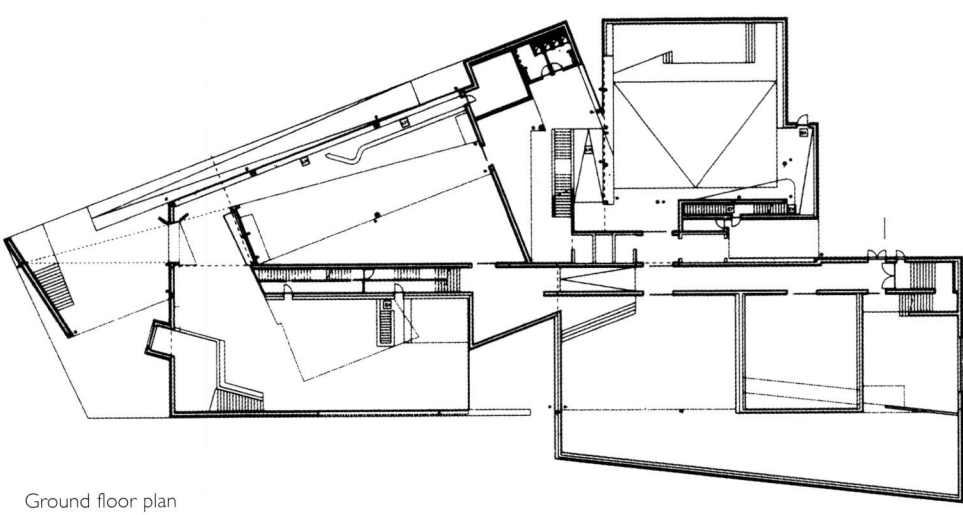

Ground floor plan

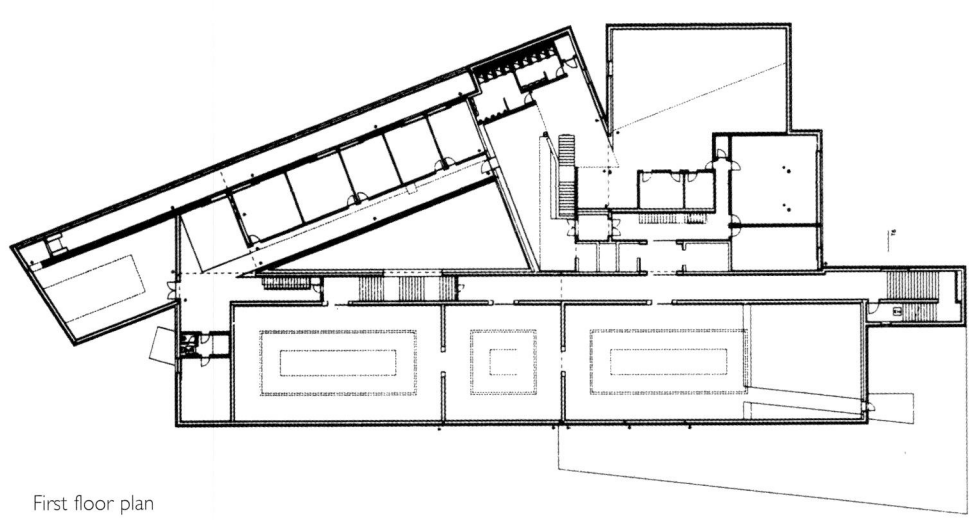

First floor plan

Antoine Predock
American Heritage Center and Art Museum

Laramie, USA

This 12,000 sqm facility was built with a budget of $13.8 million. The axis of the project is aligned with two summits - Medicine Bow Peak and Pilot's Knob in the distant Snowy Range and the nearer Laramie Range. As Predock says, this "consciously monumental landscape abstraction represents a symbol for future campus growth… and a statement of the powerful spirit of Wyoming". Situated on a 10 hectare site, the complex includes the American Heritage Center and Fine Arts Museum. The patinated copper cone at the center of the building corresponds to a nearby round basketball arena, but also calls forth images of a UFO, one of the architect's recurring themes, and is equally reminiscent of a mountainous volcanic shape or of a warrior's strange helmet.

This example illustrates Predock´s capacity to fuse sources of inspiration which can be at once geological and anchored in popular culture. The cone and its base house the American Heritage Center, a research facility for scholars. A long, terraced volume with flat roofs, trailing from the cone, houses the University of Wyoming Art Museum, with its collection of artefacts ranging from saddles to mineral maps and stills from Hollywood Westerns.

The block-like elements of the museum, intended to recall the architecture of Pueblo Indians, are built with sandblasted concrete blocks specially formed with a coarse aggregate.

Photographs: Timothy Hursley

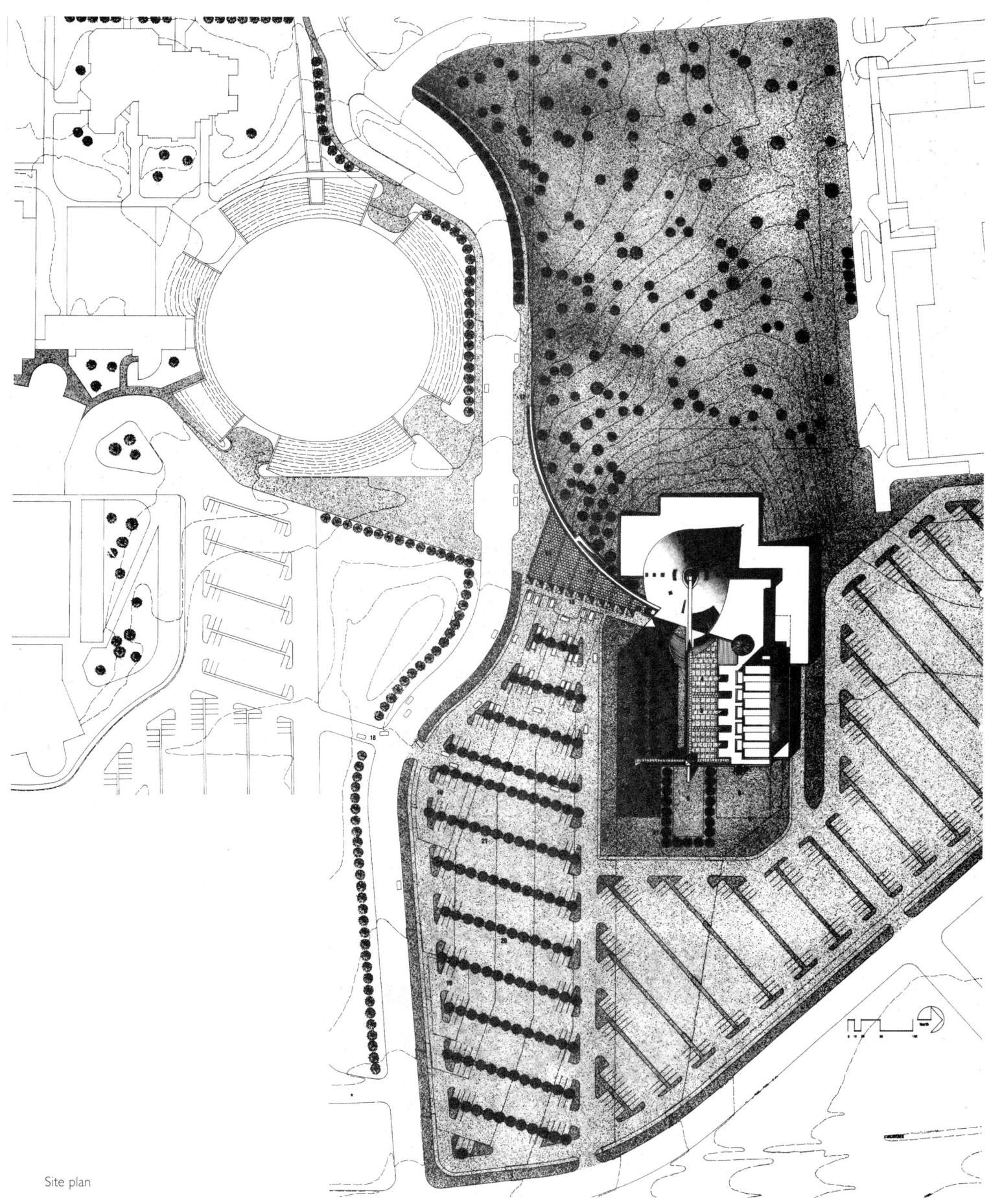

Site plan

Predock conceived the project as an abstraction, inspired by geological themes or popular culture. The complex is vaguely reminiscent of pictures of UFOs, a volcanic extrusion or perhaps, in a flight of fancy, a warrior's shield.

The American Heritage Center is built entirely of granulated reinforced concrete blocks forming simple, forceful geometric compositions that could be read as a reference to the native architecture of the Pueblo Indians.

Cross-section

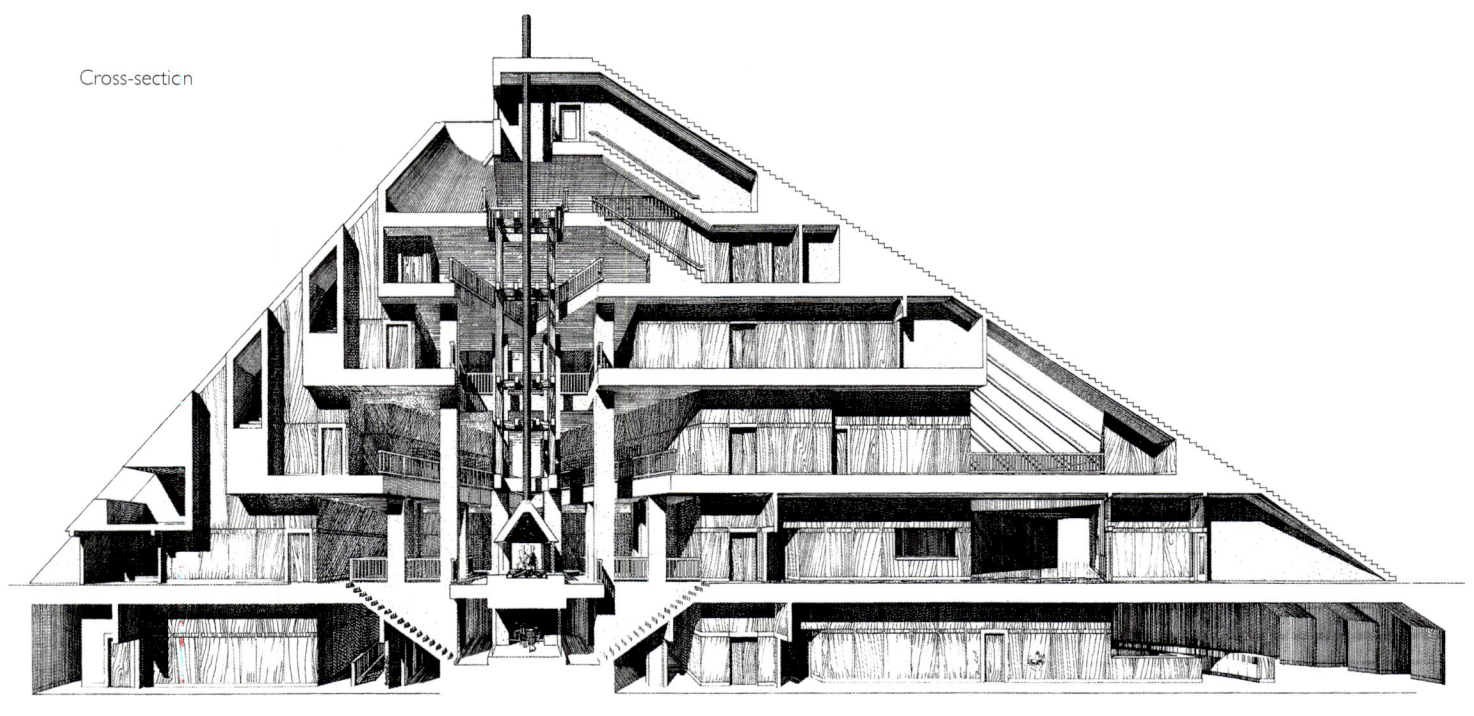

The spectacular interior spaces were formed by means of a very plastic treatment of the volumes and the architectural use of light and shade.

UN Studio van Berkel & Bos
Mercedes-Benz Museum
Facts & Figures

Stuttgart, Germany

The new Mercedes-Benz Museum, with 450,000 visitors a year, is located next to highway B14 into Stuttgart. The 16,500 m2 space contains 160 cars, a shop, a restaurant, offices, a sky lounge, and the surrounding landscape.

The Museum is trefoil shaped: three overlapping circles leave a triangular void in the center. The semi-circular floors around it form horizontal plateaus of double or single height. Several radical spatial principles are bound together, generating a completely new typology as a result. This responds partly to its museum function, partly to its peripheral urban location, and partly to concerns that belong to the discipline of architecture. The visitors proceed through the museum from top to bottom; during the ride up the atrium in one of the three elevators, visitors are shown a multimedia Preshow presentation. The elevators are like capsules with only a large slit at eye-level through which the visitor see images of the history of Mercedes-Benz, projected on the walls of the atrium.

From the eightth floor, two spiralling ramps lead back down; one connects the Legend Rooms, seconcary displays related to the history of Mercedes-Benz; the other leads to the Vehicles collection. The spirals cross like a DNA helix, allowing the visitor to choose alternative routes. The two types of museum space are diametrically opposed in character. The Legend rooms are closed and artificially lit, like a stage. The Collection rooms are open and day-lit, surrounded by huge, panoramic windows.

The building twists and turns, like a sculpture full of contrapposto; now you see things, now you don't. It will certainly take anyone several visits to figure out the building. At any point, it is difficult to know where you are precisely. The building keeps unfolding, keeps surprising you. But you cannot loose your way in this exhibition without end.

The innovative character of the museum and the limited schedule demanded an intense collaboration with the client and all the professionals involved. Digitally controlling the geometry made it possible to incorporate changes, immediately knowing the effects of that change on all other aspects of the building.

Photographs: Christian Richters, Brigida Gonzalez

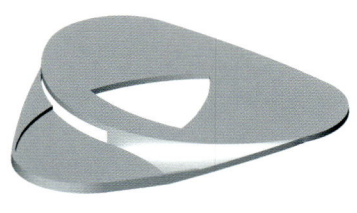

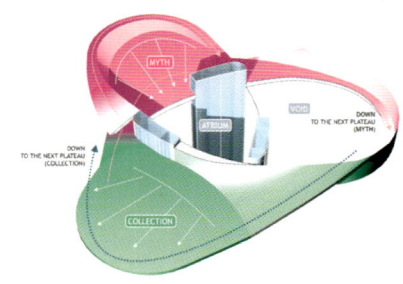

The Museum is trefoil shaped: three overlapping circles leave a triangular void in the center. The semicircular floors around it form horizontal plateaus of double or single height. Several radical spatial principles are bound together, generating a completely new typology as a result. This responds partly to its museum function, partly to its peripheral urban location, and partly to concerns that belong to the discipline of architecture.

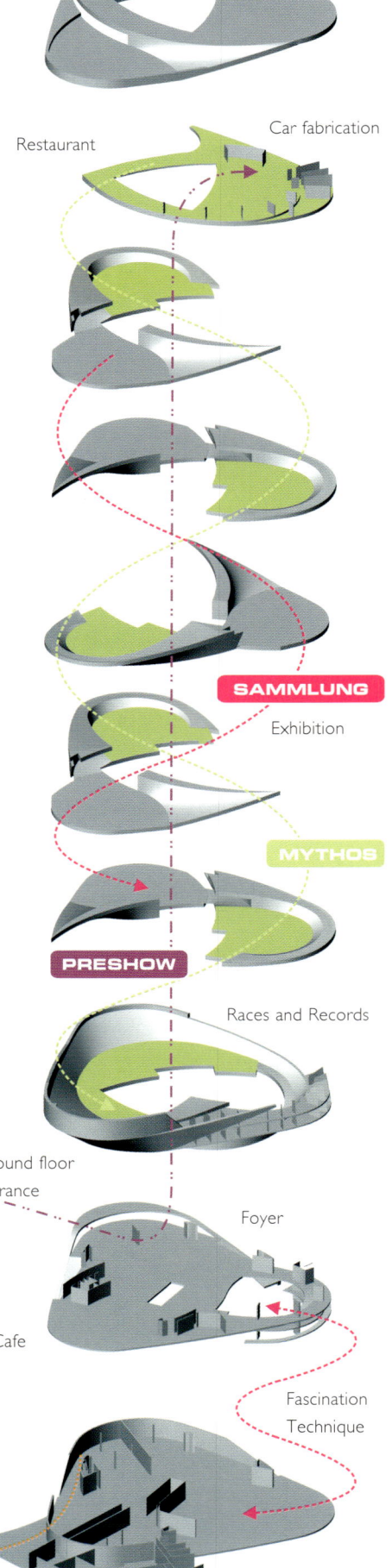

Restaurant

Car fabrication

SAMMLUNG

Exhibition

MYTHOS

PRESHOW

Races and Records

Ground floor entrance

Foyer

Cafe

Fascination Technique

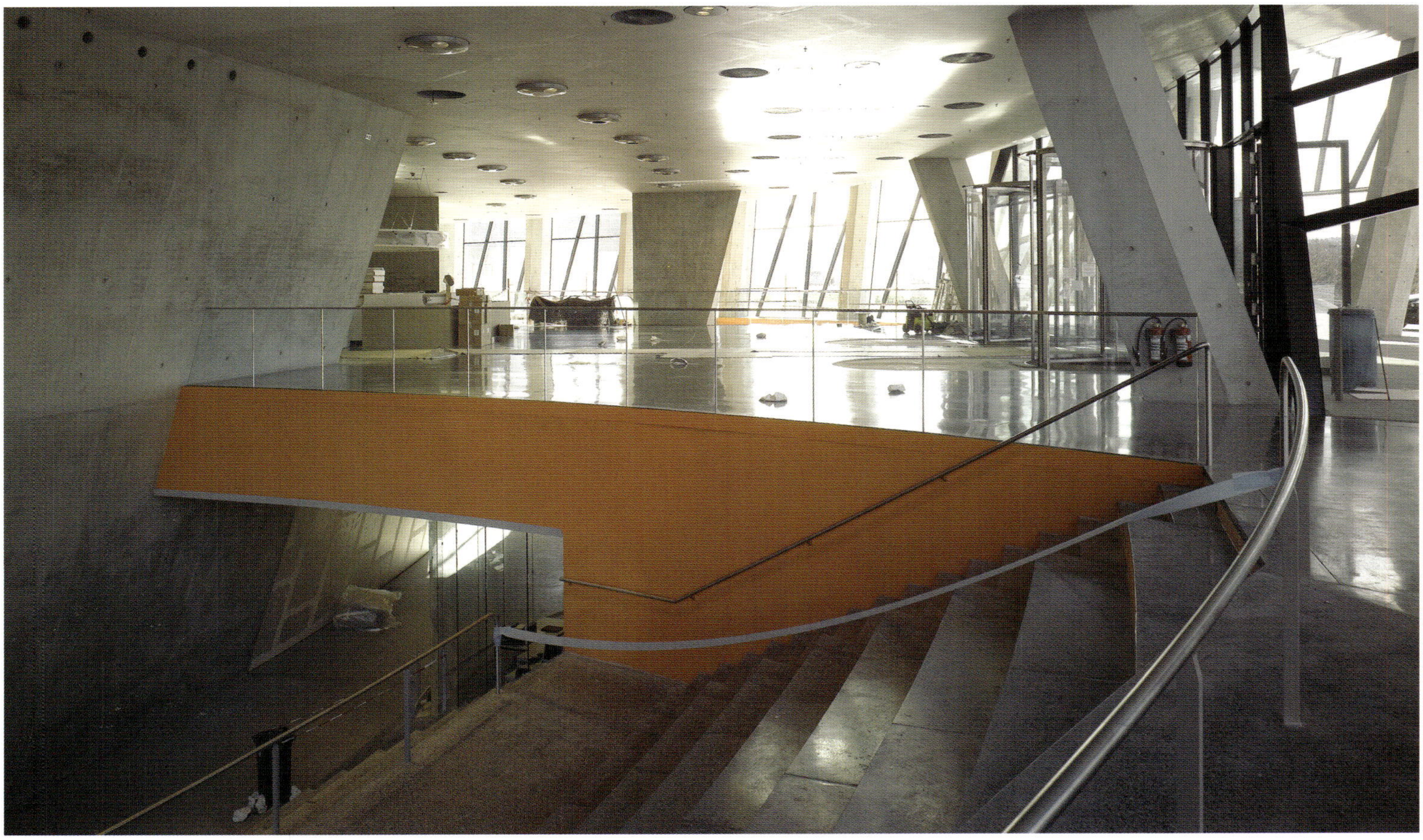

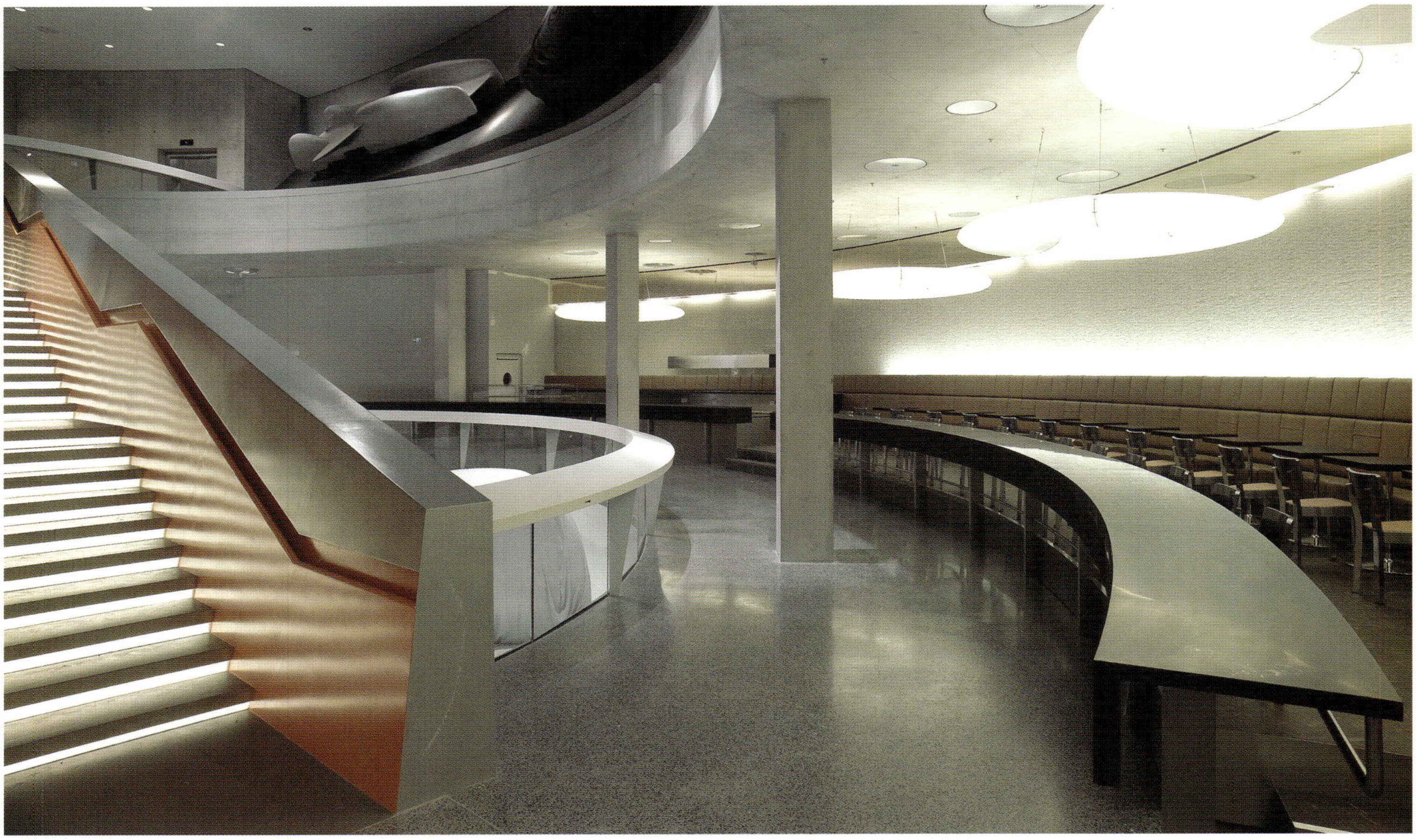

Vincent Cornu & Benoît Crépet
Museum of Ambulant Theater

Artenay, France

After the municipality of the French village of Artenay inherited some years ago the stage property of a troupe of itinerant players, it was decided to create a museum of travelling theater as the centerpiece of a whole area's renovation. Apart form the museum, the program was rounded out by a local archaeological exhibition, reserves and workshops for the museum of travelling theater, plus a documentation center and a small public library.

The architects saw this set of ordinary rural buildings as a landscape, bringing their diversity into a coherent whole and restoring an old itinerary around a new communal facility.

In order to conserve the balance of the place while asserting its new vocation, the architects magnified the walls, which they saw as vital to its identity, and manifested the presence of the new interior facilities by way of the openings.

Windows and doors were redistributed on the existing façades, restored with a careful eye for traditional stonework details. Woodwork and doorways were treated as noble elements and built by local craftsmen. The new wing, designed to close the yard of the Paradis farm that backs onto the mall, shows the same concern for unity and dialogue with neighboring forms.

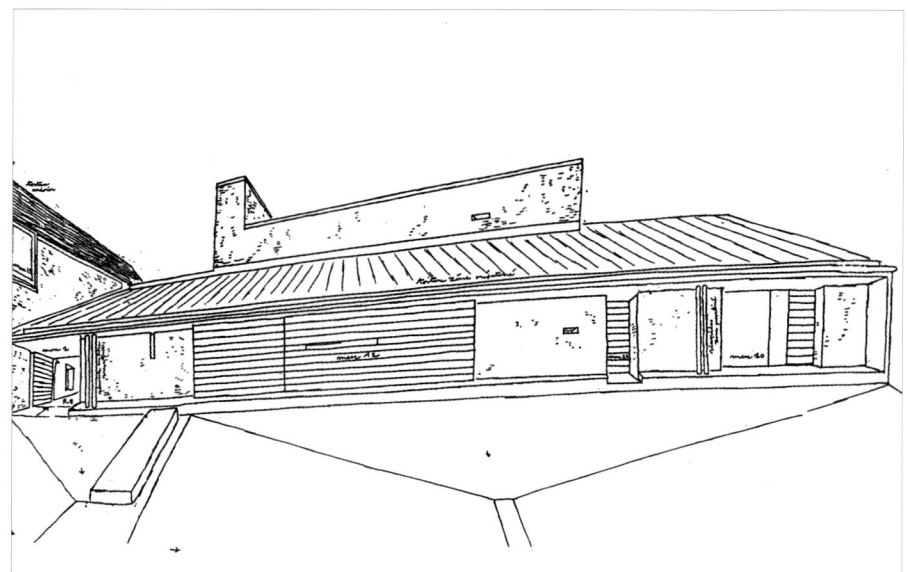

Permanent exhibition rooms are housed in what was once the main barn of the farm, the structure of which was laid bare and the rendering renovated. Linked by ramps and a footbridge, they compose a complex itinerary distributed on two levels at either side of the full-height central volume that structures the whole. Materials suggest refined rustic taste: terra cotta floors, solid woodwork, and rendering painted white to distinguish restored walls from partitions. The original door was enlarged and rebuilt with particular care. When it is open wide, the central volume is opened to nearly six meters, transforming the space into a stage for spectators gathered in the courtyard.

Photographs: Jean Marie Mothiers, Benoît Crépet

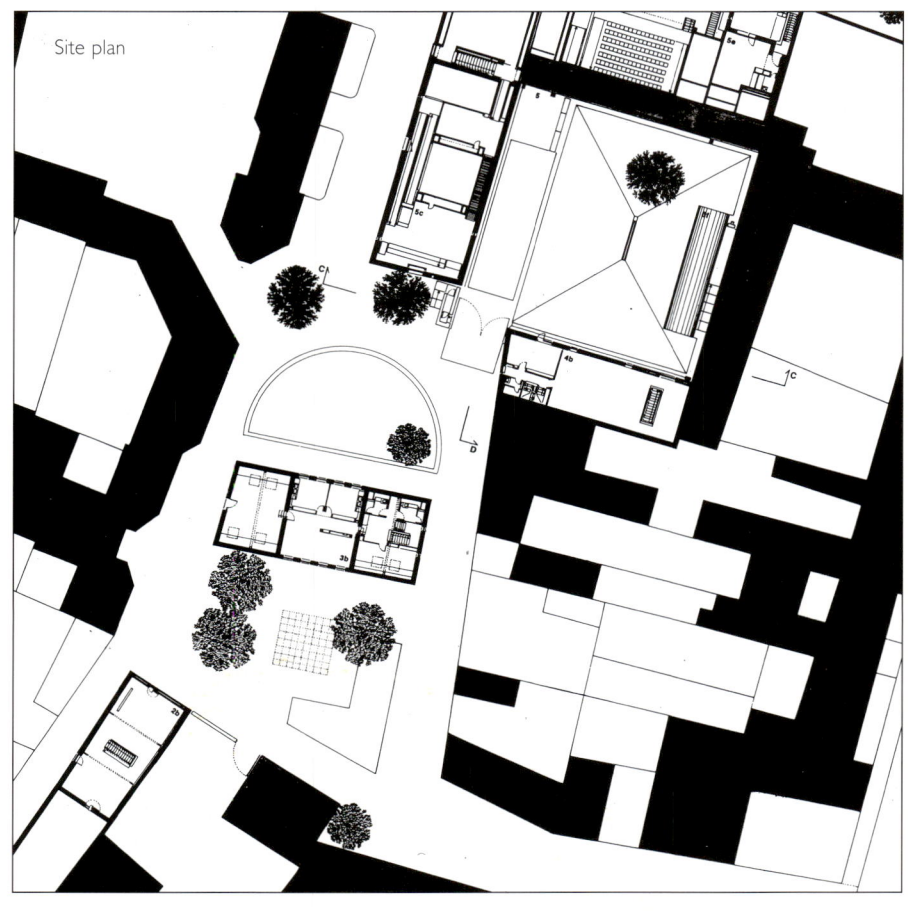

Site plan

The architectural vocabulary of the rehabilitation is attentive to the character of the place and to a knowledge of the local architecture.

The program consists of the rehabilitation of a set of buildings of agricultural origin. The vocabulary, based on the dialogue between white cloth and woodwork, seeks to unify the buildings.

The museum spaces were organized in an orderly sequence in accordance with the rhythm of life of a theatrical company at various times in history. The assembly shows elements referring to the arrival of the actors at a village, various aspects of the performance and their departure.

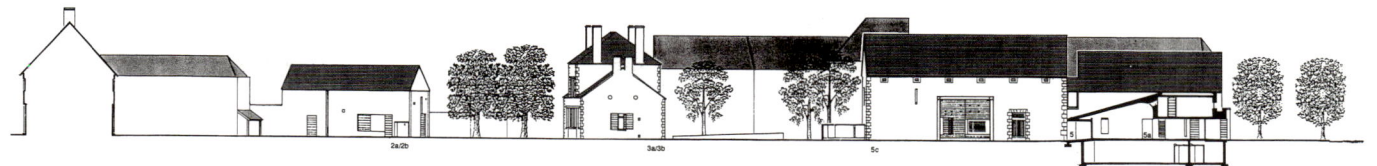

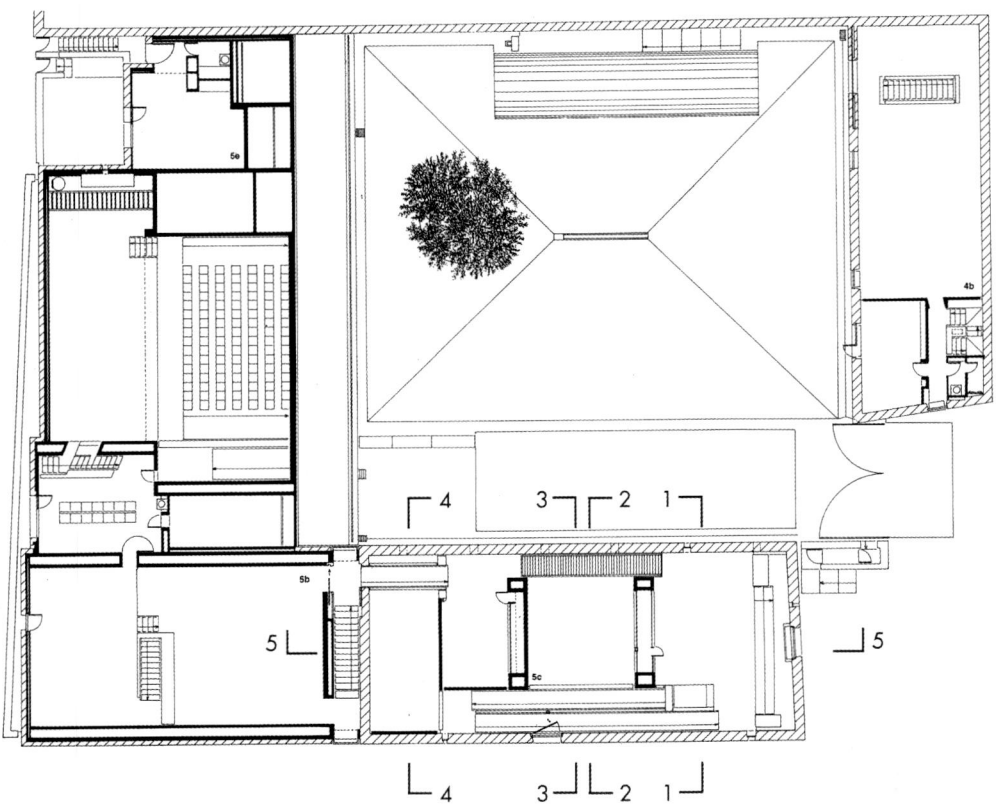

Upper floor plan

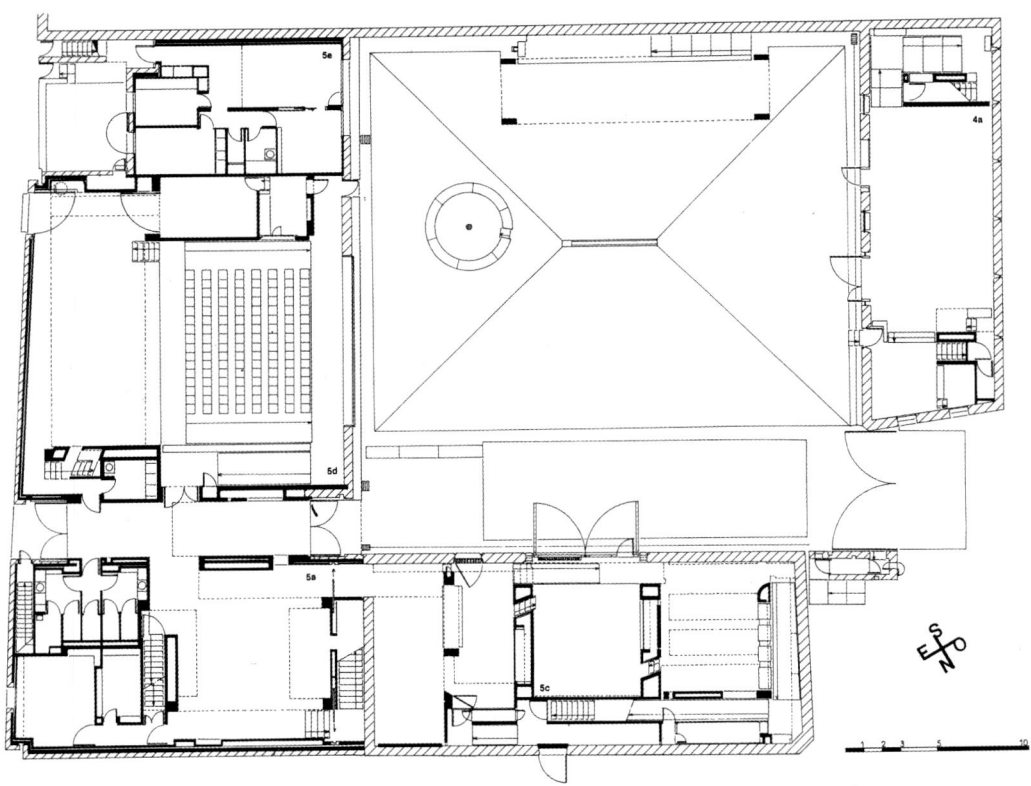

Lower floor plan

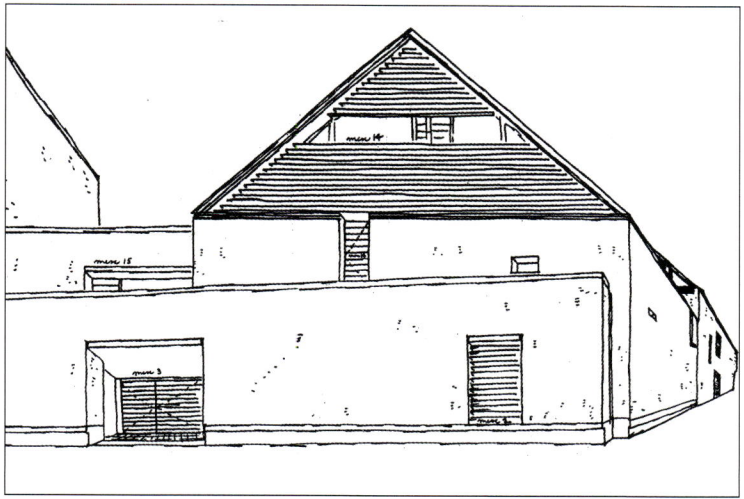

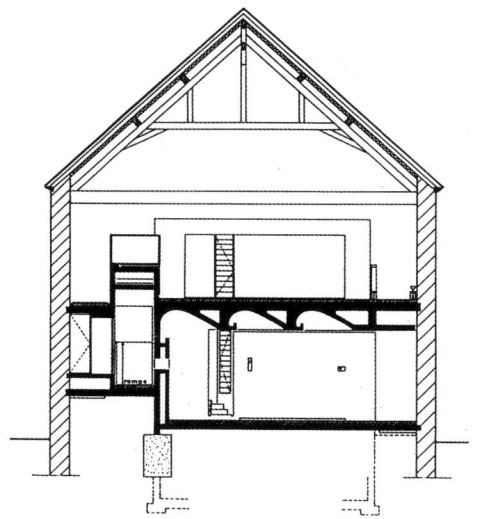

Section 1-1

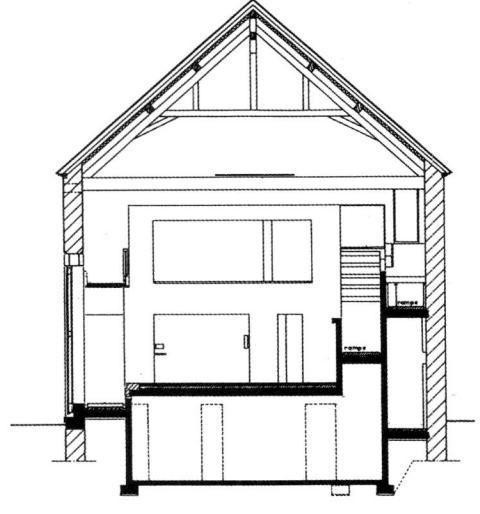

Section 2-2

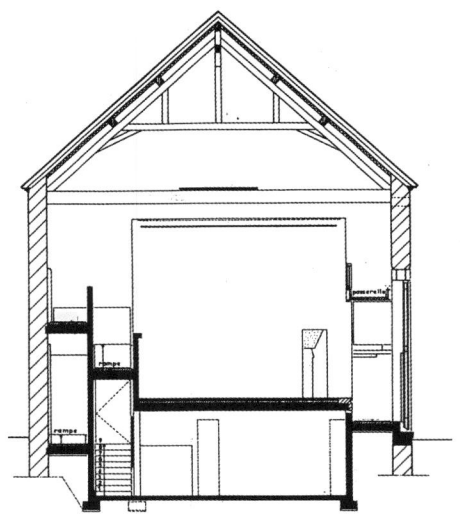

Section 3-3

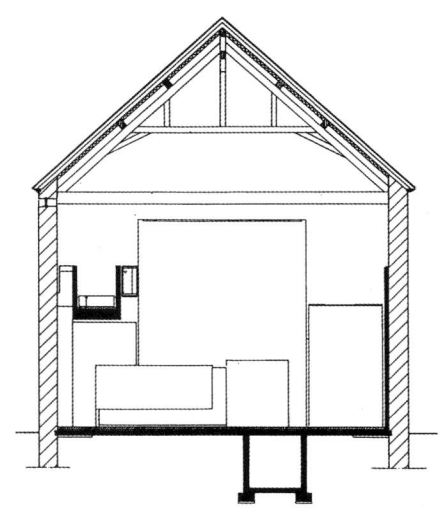

Section 4-4

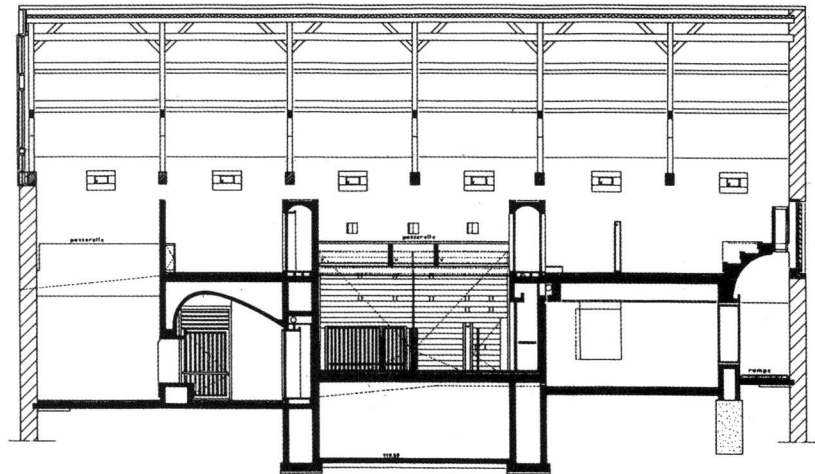

Section 5-5

Roberto Luna / Arata Isozaki
CaixaForum

Barcelona, Spain

Built between 1909 and 1911 by the architect Josep Puig i Cadafalch, the Casaramona factory was declared a national monument in 1976.

The renovation program called for its conversion into an exhibition center which, in addition to the basic exhibit spaces, would include a series of complementary rooms, such as an auditorium, media archives, halls and offices. The required surface area would be double that of the existing building.

The available space —with standardized, homogenous and versatile halls— was ideal for its conversion into exhibit halls, without having to tear anything down or undertake a major overhaul. Thus, assessment of the existing space, along with the desire to conserve it as an exhibit space and the need for more surface area, led to the central decision to house the additional functions in a new basement which would occupy the entire floor space of the factory. In order to form a coherent whole, the design for this basement was based on the existing architecture, thereby integrating the balance of the old building into the new.

In the entrance foyer, two autonomous volumes organize the space, one opaque (the reception and concierge) the other transparent (the library). The same idea of ordering the spaces through independent elements housing specific functions (translating booths, offices, bathrooms and stairwells) recurs in the rest of the building. Finishes have been resolved using veneers with no tectonic function, and with materials such as steel and glass, which comprise a contemporary space within the existing building.

By locating the new access in the basement, done by the architect Arata Isozaki, the main entrance has been exchanged for a more suitable one. A new areaway takes care of the necessary change in level and leads to the lobby, where the exhibit space is located.

The linearity and extensive use of white in the new entrance contrasts dramatically with the rest of the complex, thereby creating a rich, thought-provoking dialogue between the two architectural styles and bringing its style closer of the Mies van der Rohe Pavilion, across the street. A sculptural pergola presides over the main façade and shelters the escalator access.

Photographs: Duccio Malagamba

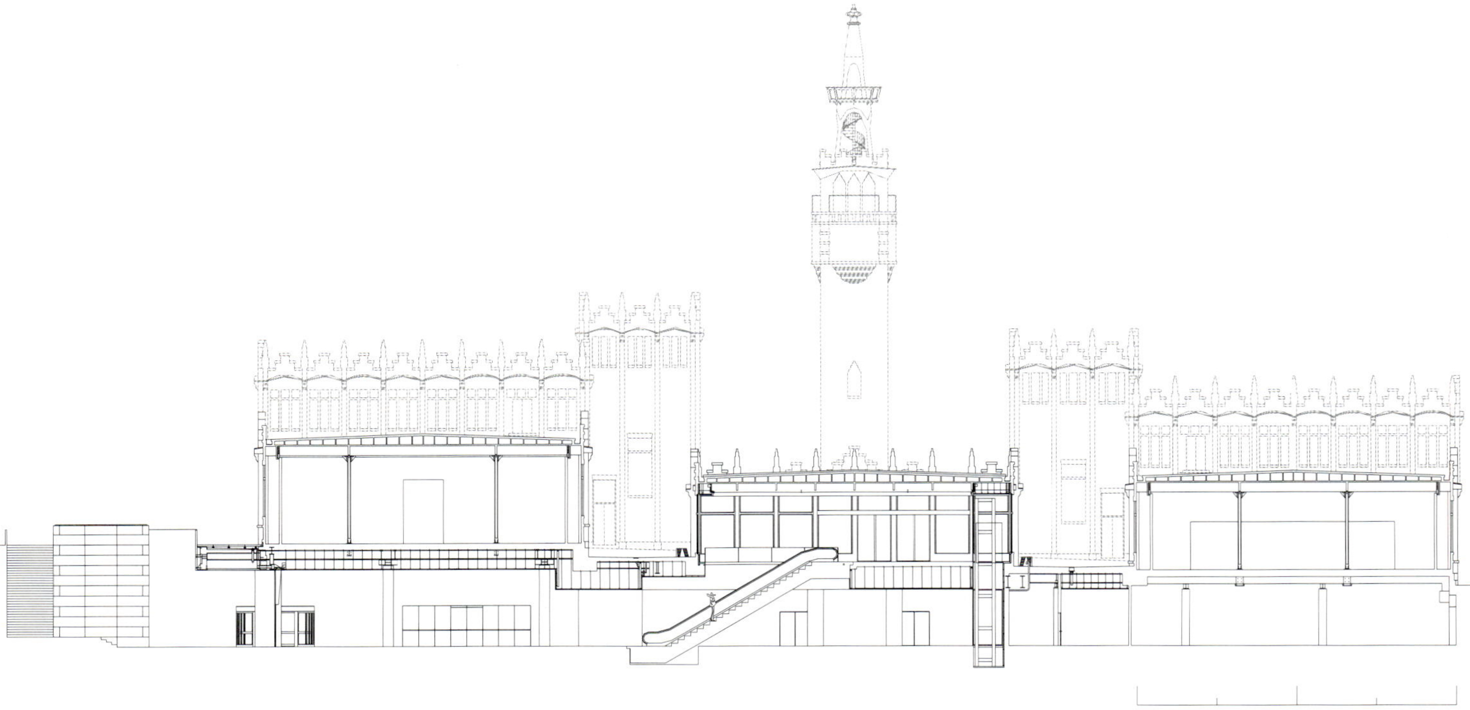

Escalator section

70

The basement translates the formal scheme of the ground floor into two large, elongated spaces (vestibule and storage) and two central areas (auditorium and media archives). The circulation zones correspond to the inner walkways of the ground floor, to which they are connected via a central nucleus of elevators and escalators and four secondary groupings.

The organization of independent bodies enabled great flexibility of use, with the inner walkways playing a central role in the formalization of the floor plan and as support for circulation between the different areas.

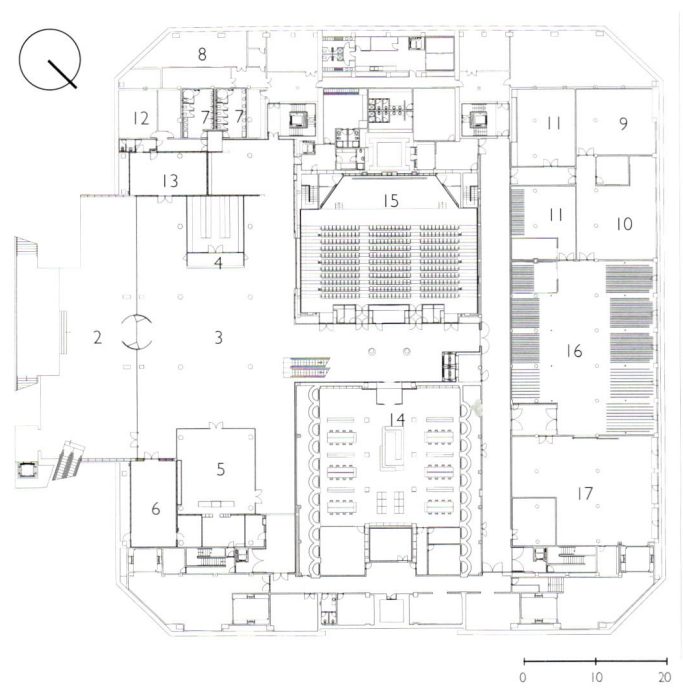

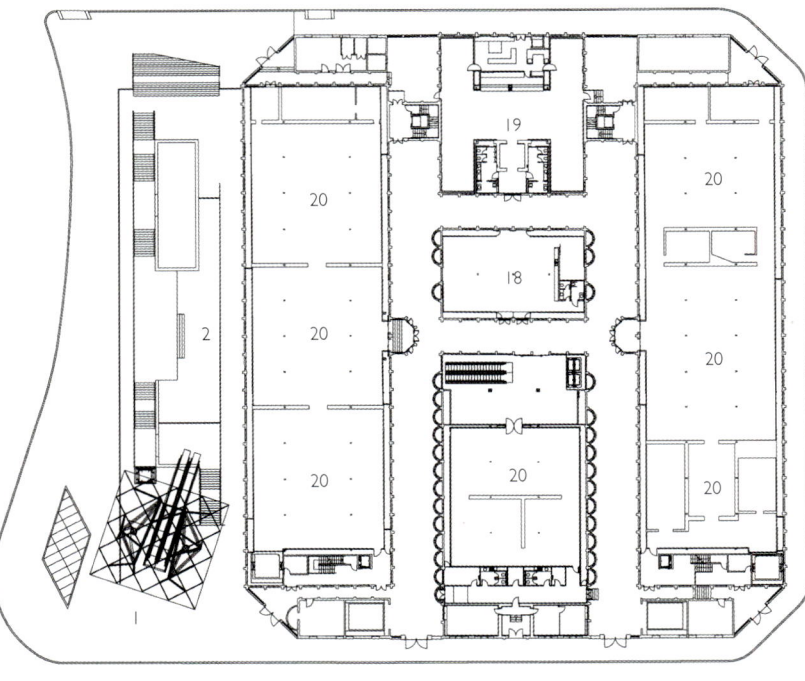

Basement floor plan

Ground floor plan

1. Access pergola
2. Open areaway
3. Hall
4. Reception and concierge
5. Shop

6. Multi-purpose hall
7. Bathroom
8. Machine rooms
9. Photography workshop
10. Restoration

11. Storage room
12. Security and control
13. VIP Room
14. Media archive
15. Auditorium

16. Storage for artwork
17. Packaging
18. Arts lab
19. Restaurant
20. Exhibit hall

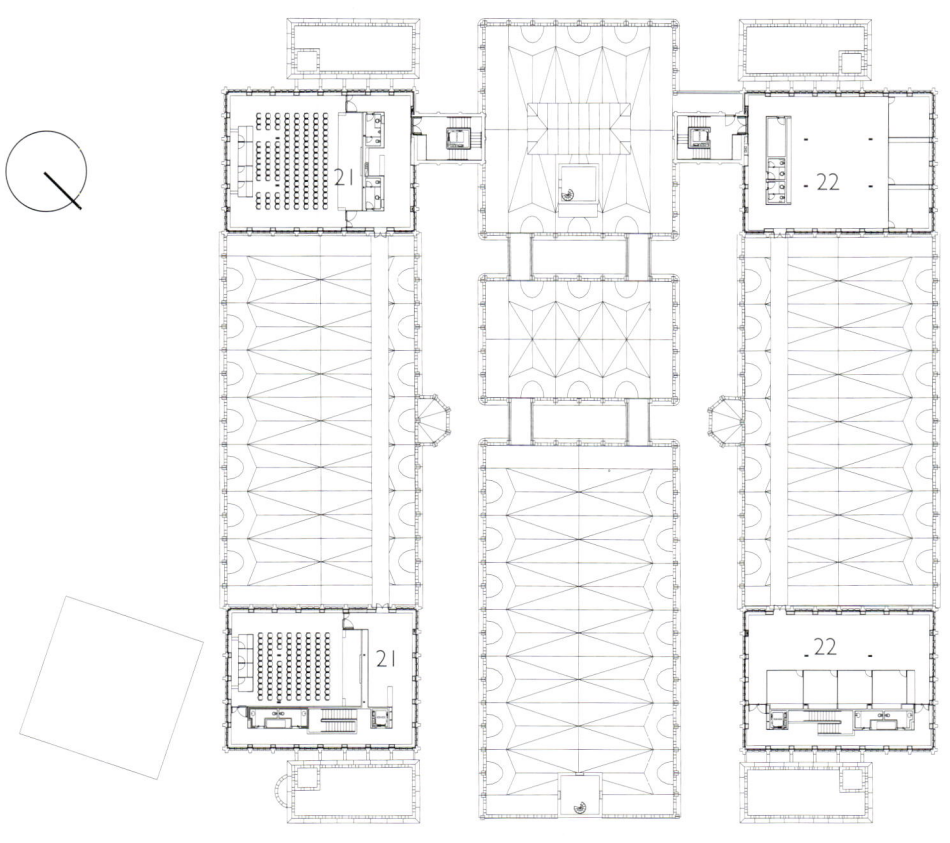

First floor plan

21. Conference room
22. Offices

0   10   20

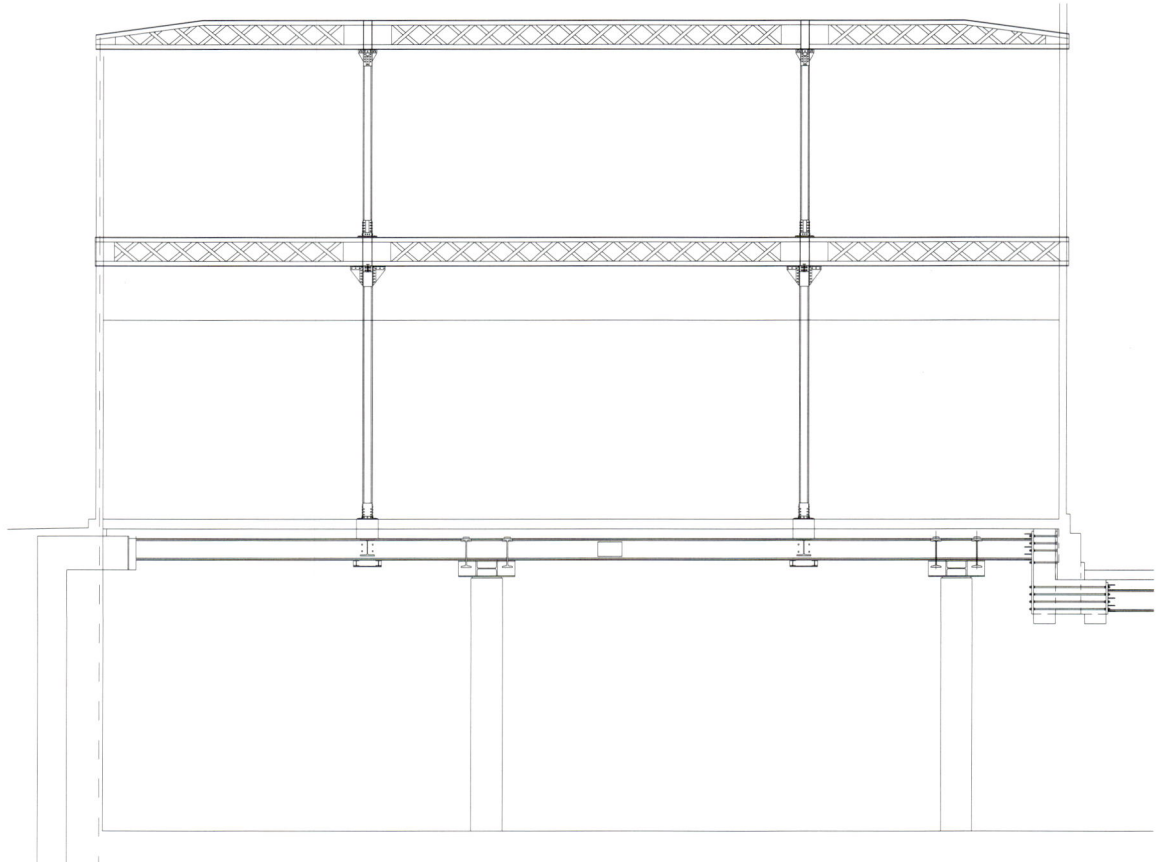

As dictated by its industrial use, the light-filled, diaphanous interior spaces were covered with a structure of metal pillars and beams, with subtle overarching vaults, giving the building its defining look.

Section of standard portico, nave B

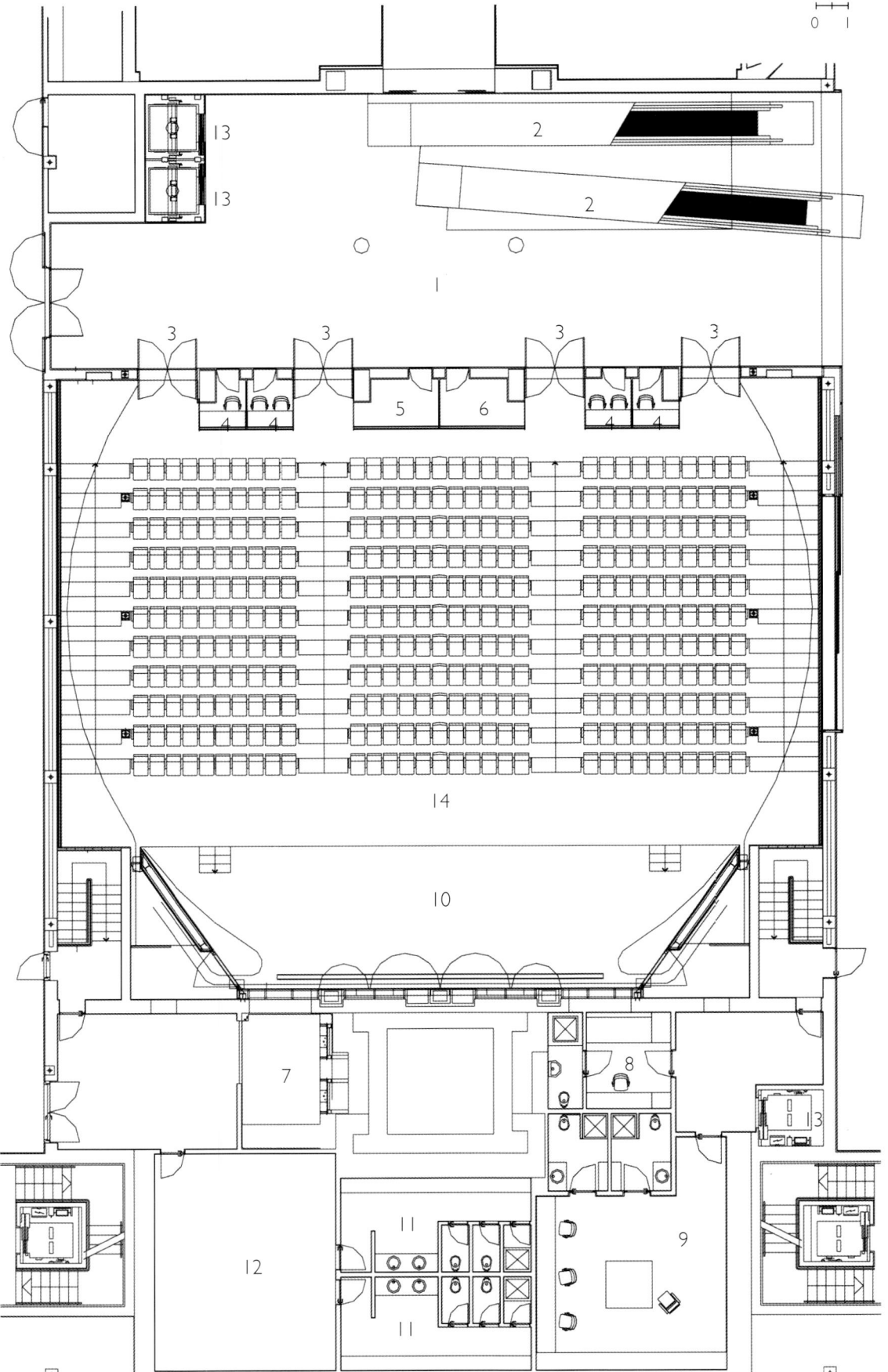

Auditorium floor plan

1. Foyer
2. Entrance escalator to exhibit room
3. Auditorium entrance
4. Translator's booth
5. Screening room
6. Sound room
7. Service elevator
8. Individual dressing room
9. General dressing room
10. Stage
11. Bathroom
12. Dressing room
13. Elevator
14. Auditorium seating

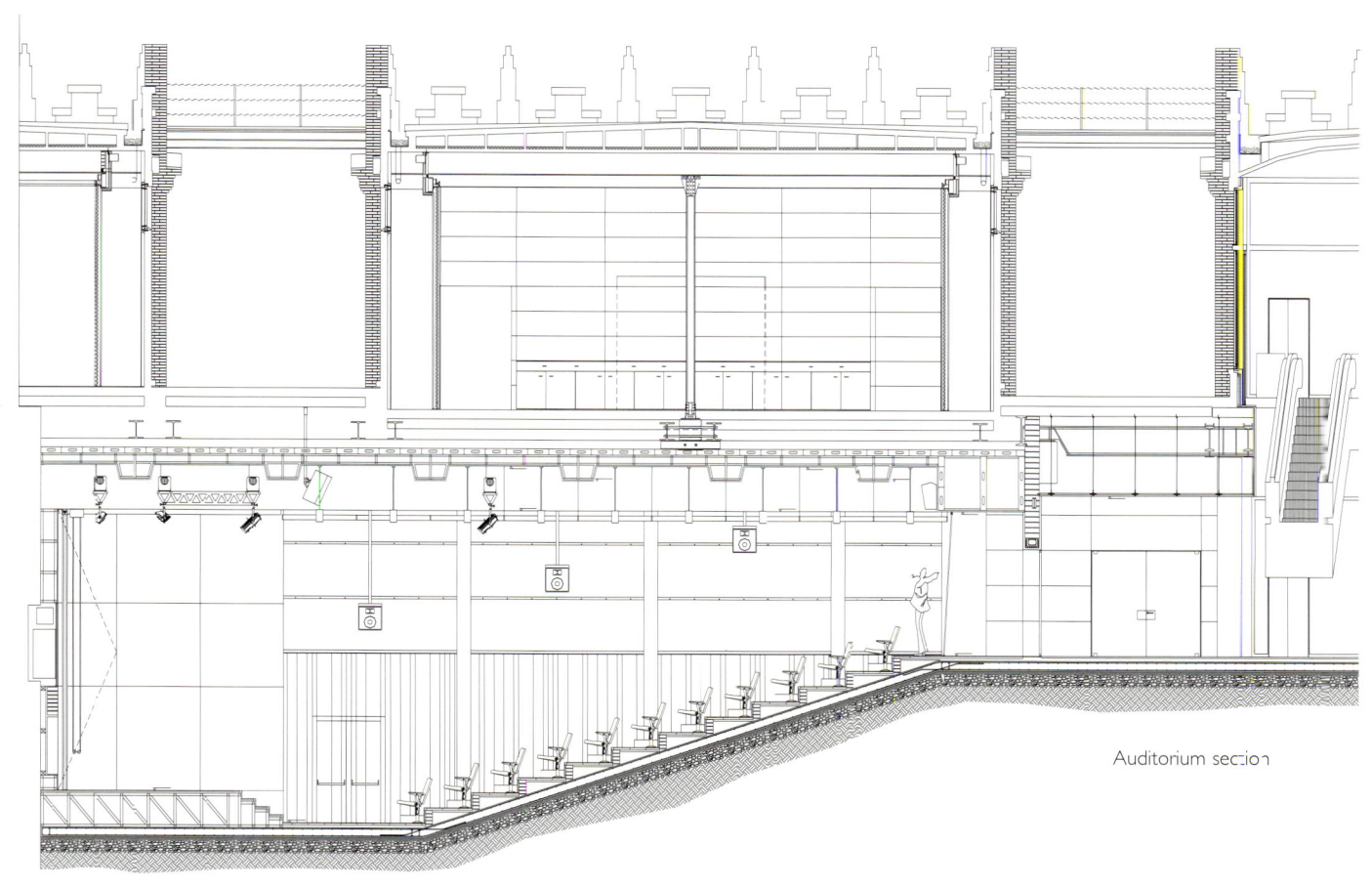

Auditorium section

Gigon / Guyer architects + Zulauf Seippel Schweingruber, landscape architects
Museum and Park Kalkriese

Kalkriese, Germany

The site for this commission is an agricultural parcel (approx. 20 Ha) that is considered to be the long-sought location of the famous battle of the Teutons against the Romans in the year 9 A.D.: the Battle of Varus.

The probable course of the Roman legion's route along the rampart has been retraced by means of large, irregularly placed iron plates laid out along the ground, comprising a footpath. These plates are engraved with historical, Roman and contemporary written fragments. Proceeding from iron plate to iron plate and collecting fragments of information (like archeologists) from the ground, an image of the historical battle situation develops step by step within the visitor's minds. By contrast, narrow paths strewn with wood chips form a net-like pattern that represents the Teuton's positions in the forest.

The location and assumed height of the former Teutonic earthen rampart, including palisades built on top, have been marked by means of iron poles. Where archeological proof of the rampart's existence is at hand, the iron bars have been placed more closely together. Where they have been placed farther apart, the location of the earlier ramparts is open to speculation.

Landscape design measures aimed at visualizing the original site (course of the terrain, make-up of the ground) were simply realized with contemporary farming machinery. The existing forest has been supplemented with trees to the south in order to trace its former edge. To the north, it was partially cleared to form fields in order to render the expanse of the former moor landscape.

Three pavilions (centered on the themes of seeing, hearing and questioning) on the field both broaden and put into perspective the impressions gained outdoors.

The museum consists of a one-story volume and a tower-like structure. The actual exhibition is to be found in the torso of the building, where a darkened, undivided room allows for the unfettered staging of the manifold themes of this battle.

As a functional supplement to the museum and park, an existing farm has been converted into a visitor's center, with a restaurant, children's museum, conference rooms, and offices for both the administration and the archeologists. The latter will continue to excavate and conduct research into the battle ground in the coming years, contributing new finds and insights, and thus continuing to write the history of the battle.

Photographs: Heinrich Helfenstein

Site plan

1. Former farm (now annexed to museum)
2. Museum
3. Parking
4. Roman road
5. Cheruscan line
6. The ''questioning'' pavilion
7. The ''hearing'' pavilion
8. The "seeing" pavilion
9. Excavation of original topography

The probable course of the Roman legion's route along the rampart has been retraced by means of large irregularly placed iron plates, each of which is inscribed with historical or contemporary information, thus guiding visitors through the battle site. Other path networks are delineated by wood chips and gravel.

The "hearing" pavilion is equipped with a large pipe that transmits the amplified sounds of the outside world into a soundproofed room. Inside, a pipe can be turned by hand and directed toward exterior sources of sounds.

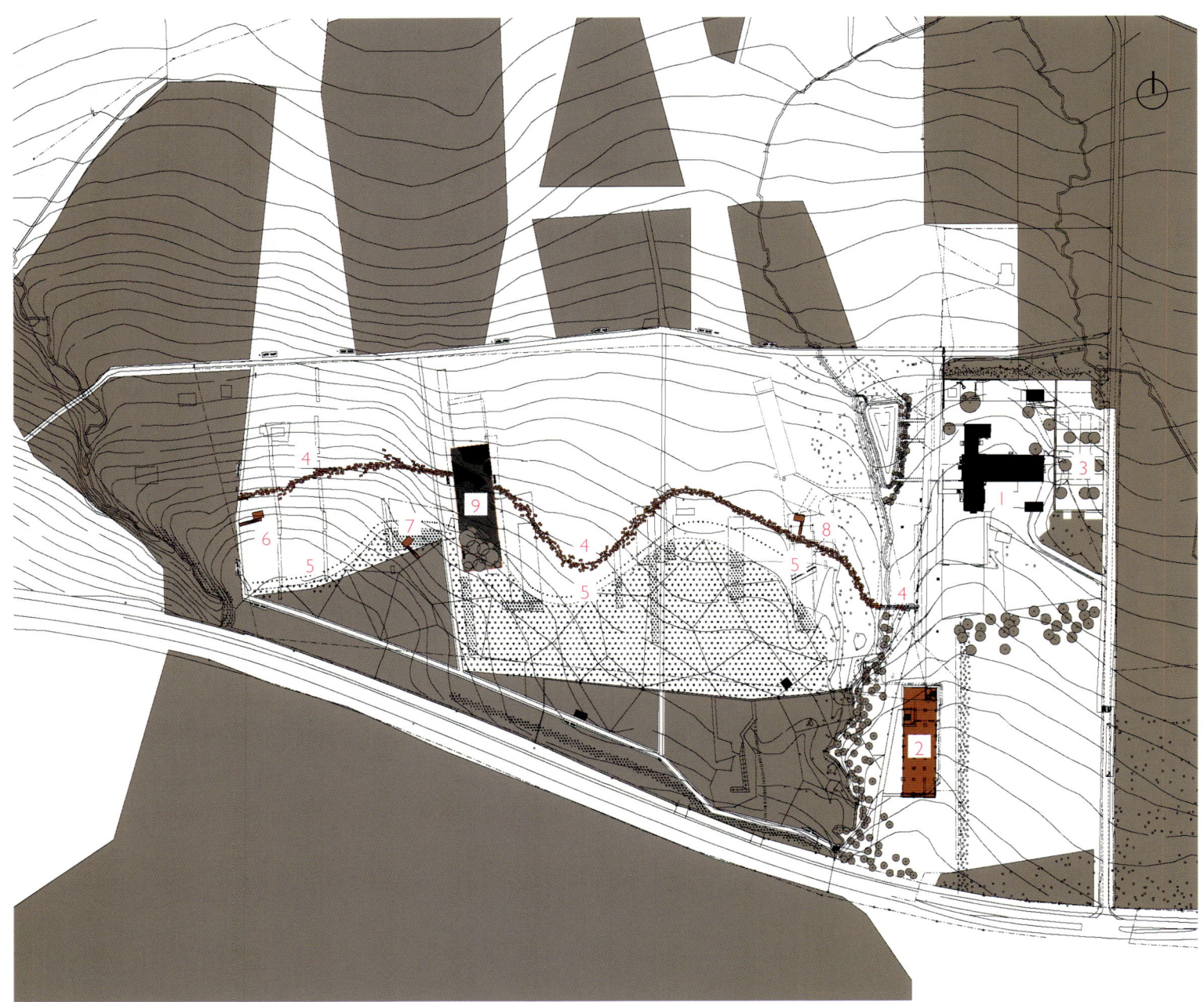

The "hearing" pavilion

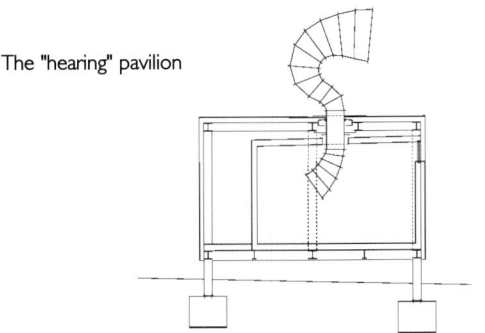

Section

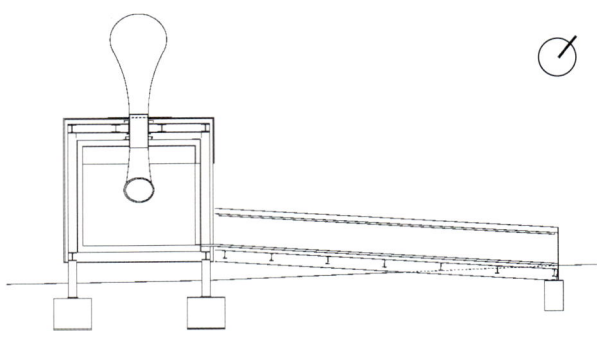

Longitudinal section

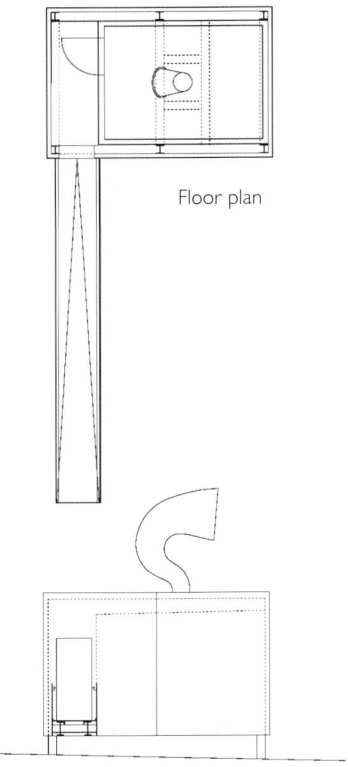

Floor plan

Roof plan

South-East Elevation

South-West Elevation

The "seeing" pavilion

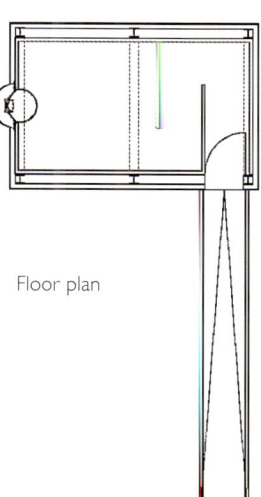

Floor plan

0   4m

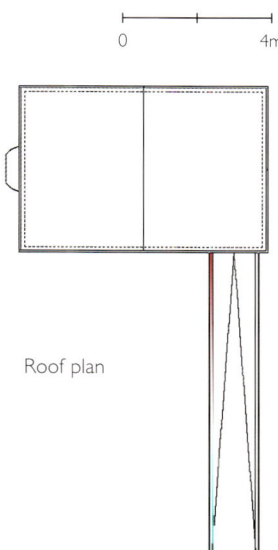

Roof plan

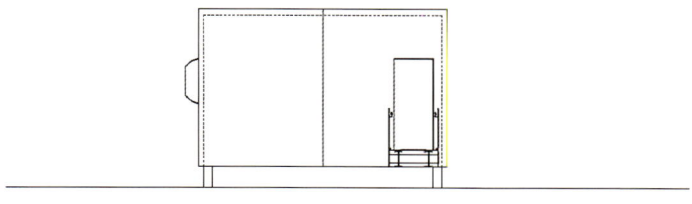

South Elevation

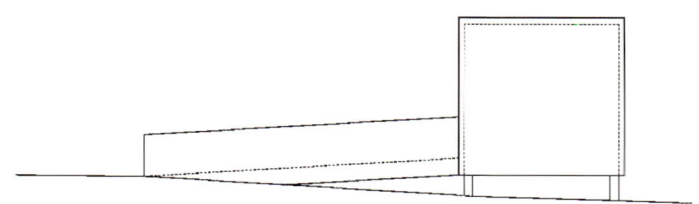

East Elevation

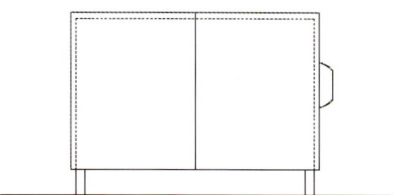

North Elevation

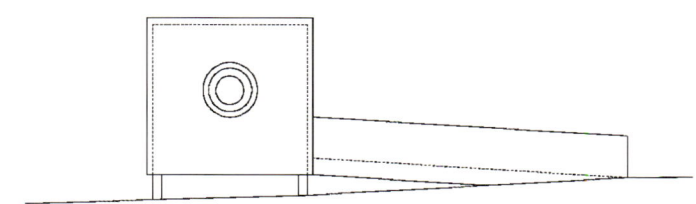

West Elevation

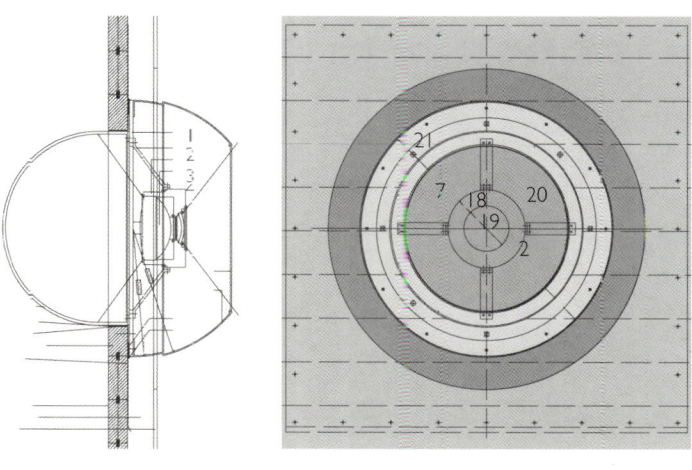

Construction detail of the "seeing" pavilion's eye

The "questioning" pavilion

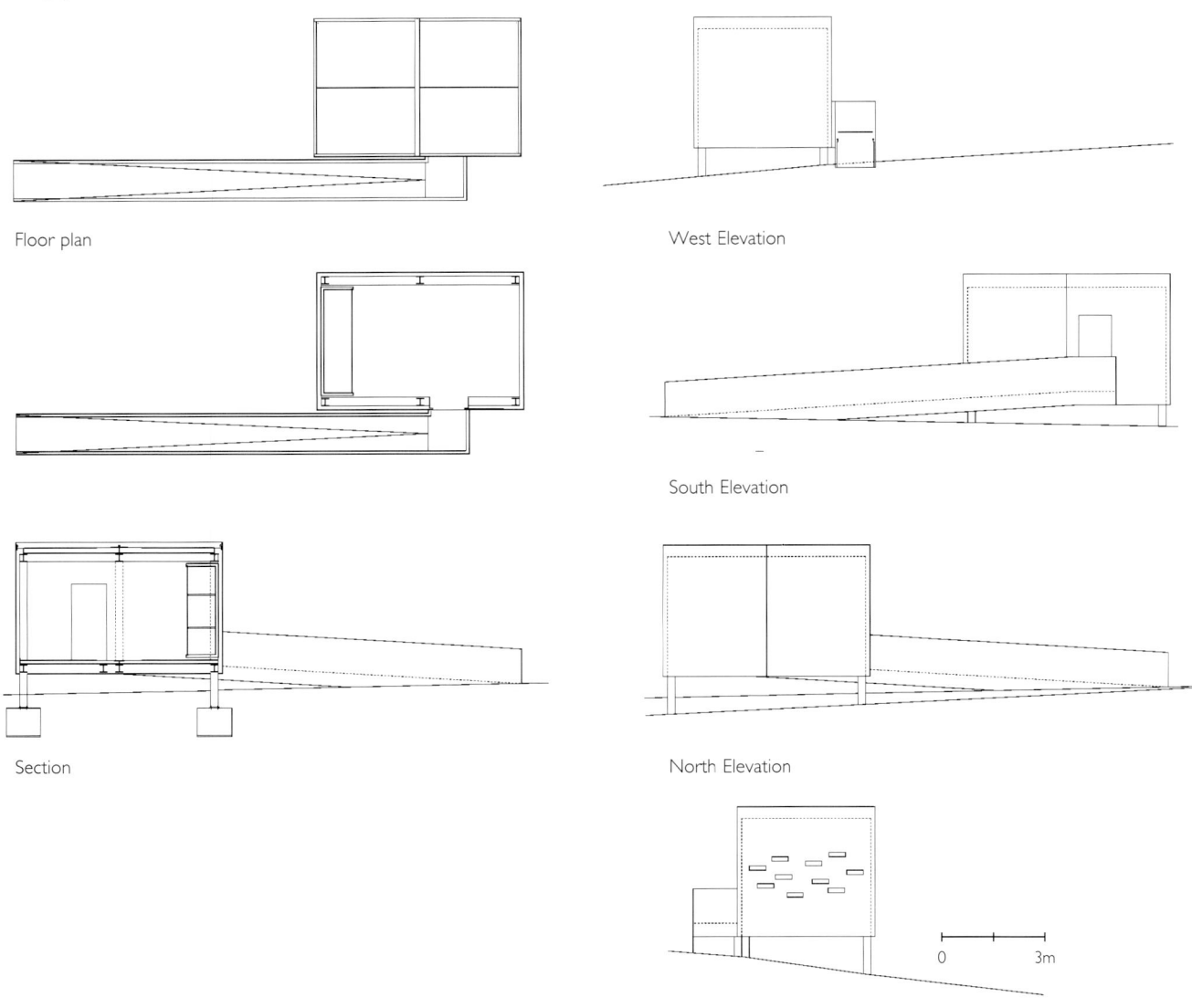

Floor plan

West Elevation

South Elevation

Section

North Elevation

East Elevation

0   3m

1. Support ring external radius = 530mm, internal radius = 340 mm
2. Crosspieces, 4 pieces
3. Lens frame
4. Objective with four lenses
5. Glass with solar protection, used according to assembly, detachable
6. Roof, protection from climatic conditions, 6 mm hot galvanized steel, external radius = 540mm
7. 5-8mm compression band

8. Long-lasting elasticized hermetic sealant
9. Sandblasted plexiglass, d=12mm, external radius = 400mm
10. Long-lasting elasticized hermetic sealant
11. 5-8mm compression band
12. Wood massing elements: d=80mm
13. Plate, d=1.5mm black matte cladding, with drip-proof edge, affixed to wood-

en structure, sealed with silicone, in situ dap d=810mm after assembly of steel face (as with wood construction)
14. Black matte layer
15. Ventilation system, d=110mm
16. Sandblasted sheets of steel, 15mm
17. Glass with solar protection
18. Lens frame
19. Optics system
20. Crosspieces
21. Support ring

22. Roof, protection from climatic conditions
23. Wood support
24. Plexiglass
25. Plate, d=1.5mm black matte cladding, with drip-proof edge, affixed to wood-en structure, sealed with silicone, in situ dap d=810mm after assembly of steel face (as with wood construction)

The "seeing" pavilion features a camera obscura that projects upside-down images of the exterior world onto a glowing half-sphere. Akin to the function of the human eyeball, what one sees is projected upon this over-sized, glass "retina". Without electricity, this glass half-sphere casts a mystical glow into the darkened room.

Inside the "questioning" pavilion, a wall with slit-like openings faces a wall with nine television monitors, where a compilation of current news broadcasts show how, to this day, conflicts continue to be fought with aggression and violence.

Museum. Floor plan -1   Floor plan 0   Floor plan +1

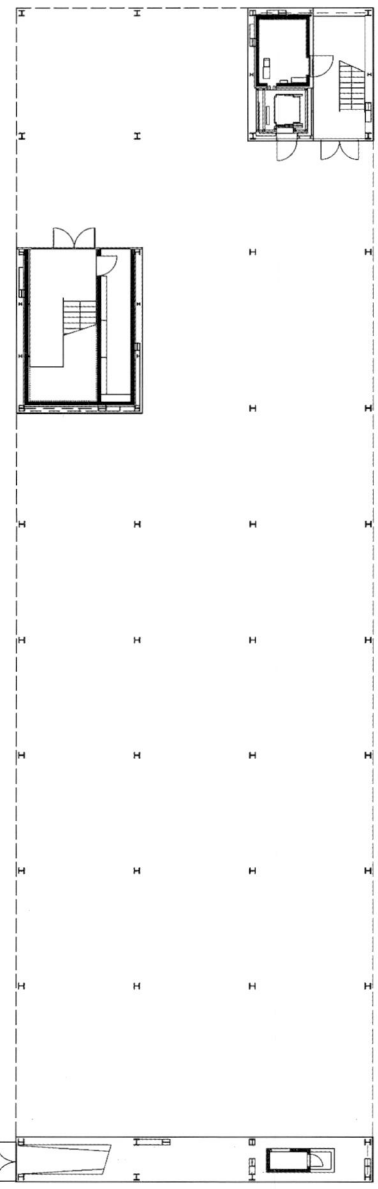
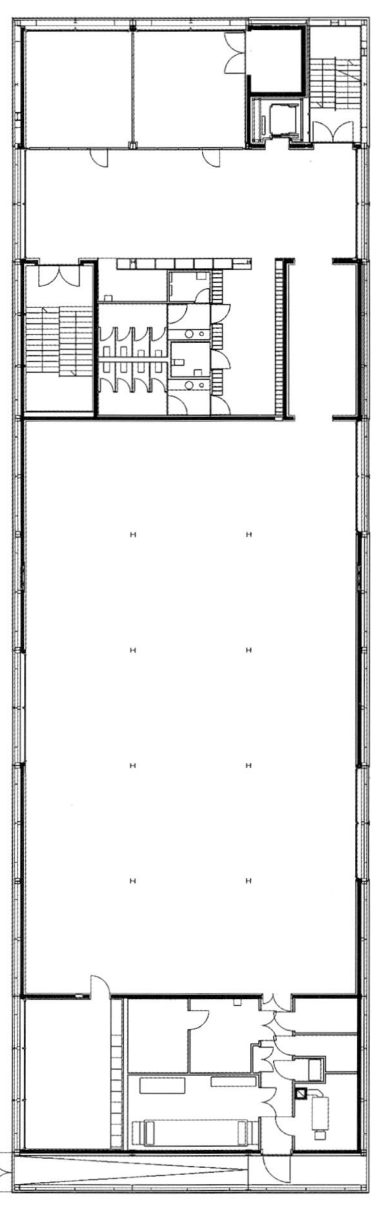
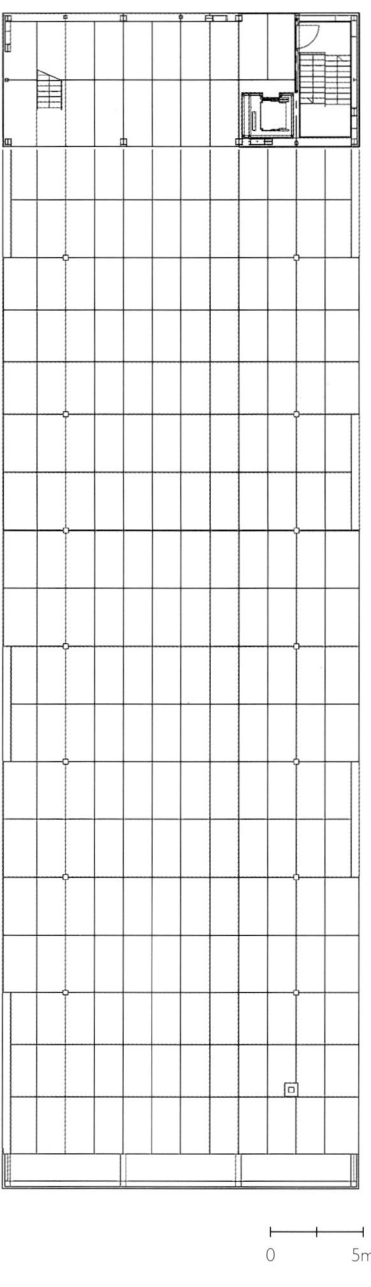

0   5m

The museum consists of a one-story volume and a tower-like structure. The landscape and the one-time battlefield can be taken in with a bird's eye view from nearly 40 meters above the ground. Like the pavilions, the museum is constructed with a steel skeleton and clad with large, rusting steel plates. Steel plates have also been used within the heated interior part of the museum as cladding (rolled steel plates for the wall and ceiling and non-rusting steel for the floor plates).

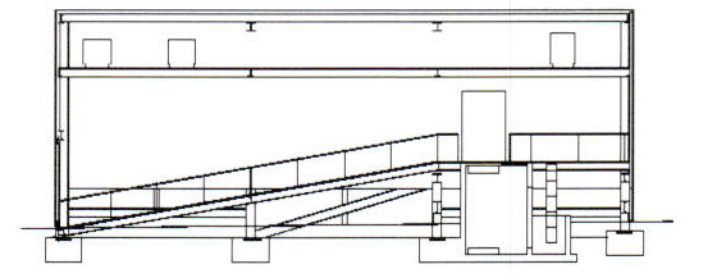

Section AA

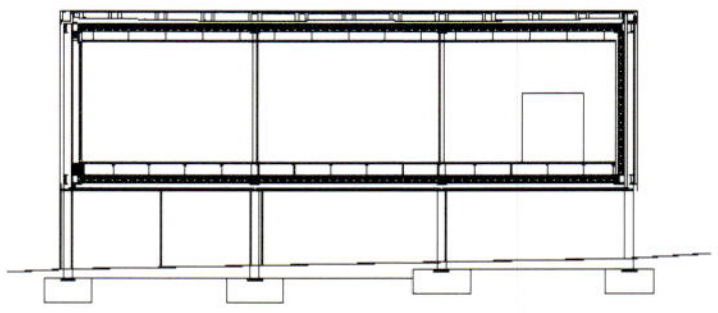

Section BB

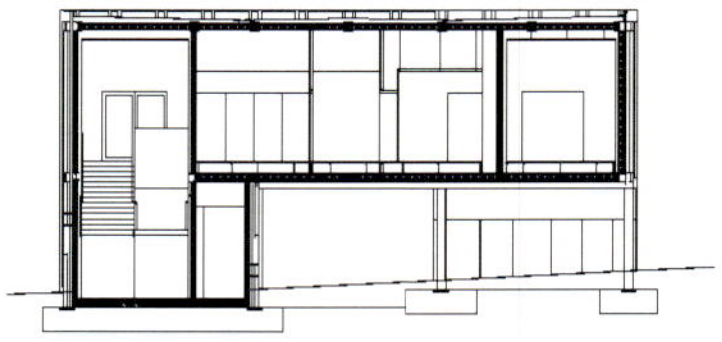

Section CC

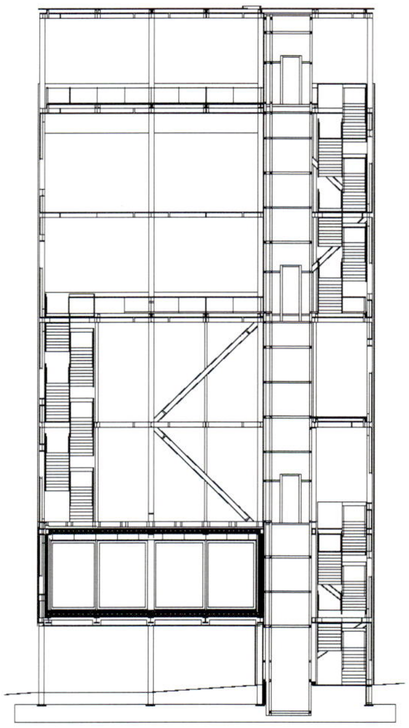

Section DD

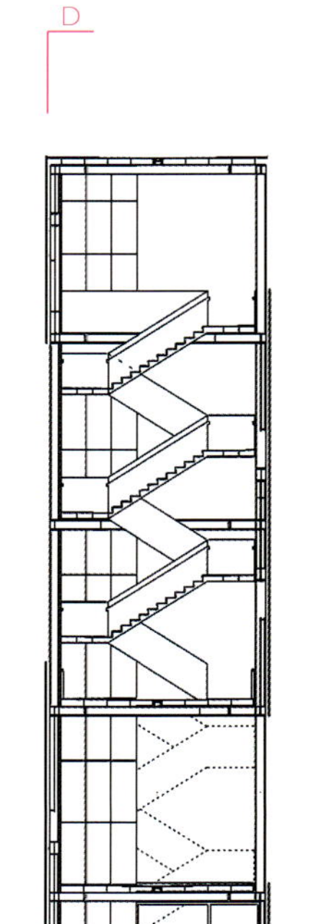

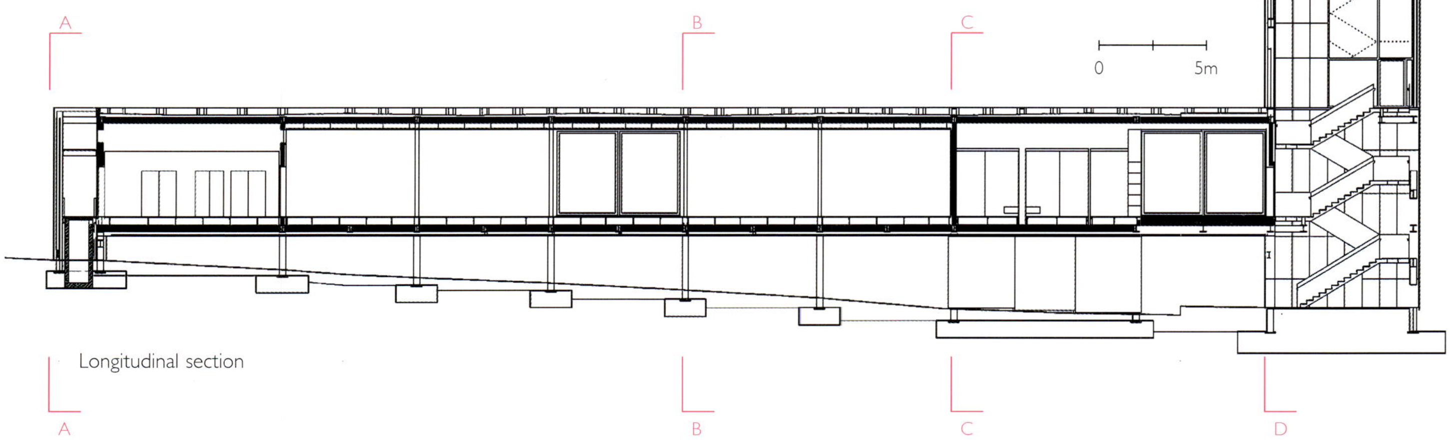

A   B   C

0   5m

D

Longitudinal section

A   B   C   D

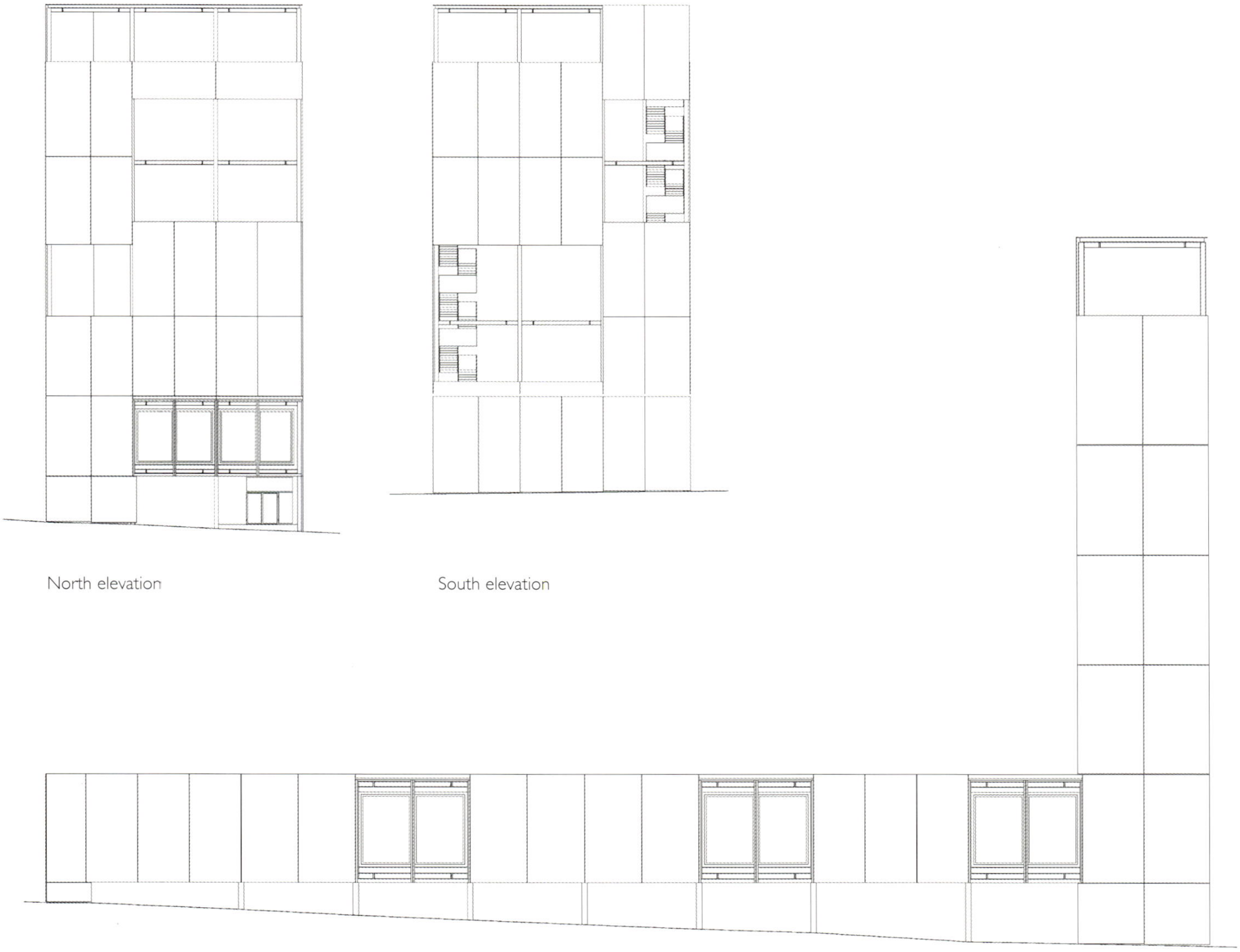

North elevation

South elevation

East elevation

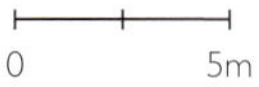

0   5m

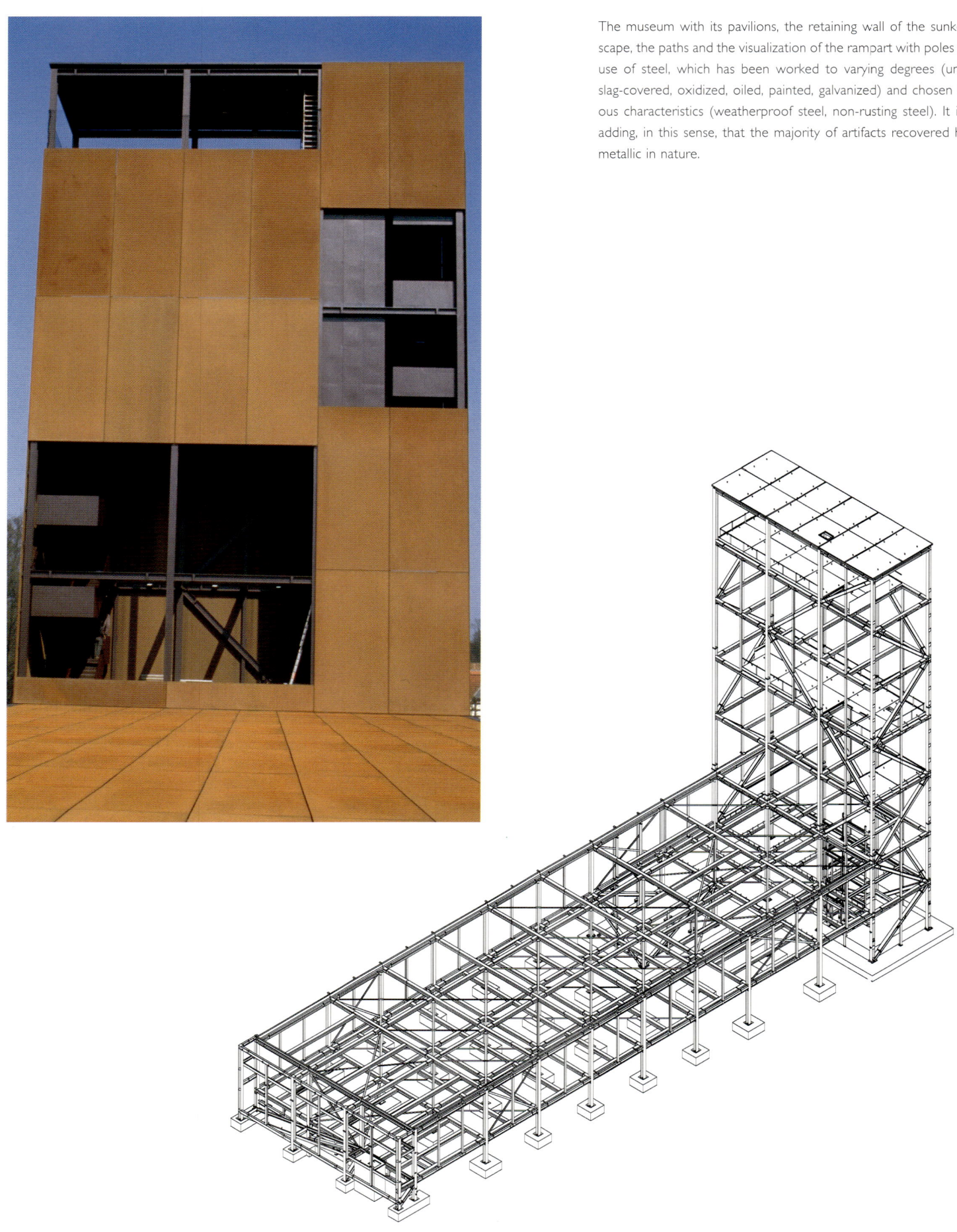

The museum with its pavilions, the retaining wall of the sunken landscape, the paths and the visualization of the rampart with poles all make use of steel, which has been worked to varying degrees (untreated, slag-covered, oxidized, oiled, painted, galvanized) and chosen for various characteristics (weatherproof steel, non-rusting steel). It is worth adding, in this sense, that the majority of artifacts recovered here are metallic in nature.

Tadao Ando
Awaji-Yumebutai

Awajishima, Hyogo, Japan

On January 17, 1995, Awaji Island was the epicenter for a massive earthquake that shook the region around Kobe and claimed more than 6000 lives. The construction documents for Yumebutai were nearly complete when the disaster struck and, eventually, the architectural team ended up re-creating construction documents in order to re-conceive Yumebutai as both a physical and spiritual rebuilding of the devastated cities - a symbol of rebirth.

Yumebutai is a complex of overlapping, intersecting, multi-directional, linear, circular and irregular spaces, including an international conference hall, a hotel, a "shell" beach with 1,000,000 scallop shells embedded in the ground, various gardens and plazas, a greenhouse and an outdoor theater. One specific item that did change after the quake was the addition of a series of terraced flower gardens called "100 Step Garden", built in remembrance of the victims of that disaster.

The construction site at the start of the project was the scarred remains of a quarry, which had been gouged out and used in the construction of a huge landfill site for the Osaka Bay area. Yumebutai began with the idea of taking land that had been destroyed through human intervention and restoring and reforesting it to life, again through human intervention. Beginning in 1994, 250,000 saplings were planted on its 30-degree slope.

Even before any architectural construction, the creation of small woodlands was the first step in an attempt towards the ideal. Development would not be premised on the destruction of nature, but rather the opposite: the project would restore nature to an area scarred by past development and would create a new place in the area for people to gather and interact.

Photographs: Mitsuo Matsuoka

The terraced Hyakudan-en Gardens are arranged on the slope of the hill where the hotel was originally to be placed. After the earthquake, a fault line was found to run directly beneath the site, making it impossible to build a hotel there. This garden was created instead to commemorate the 6000 victims of the earthquake.

Site plan

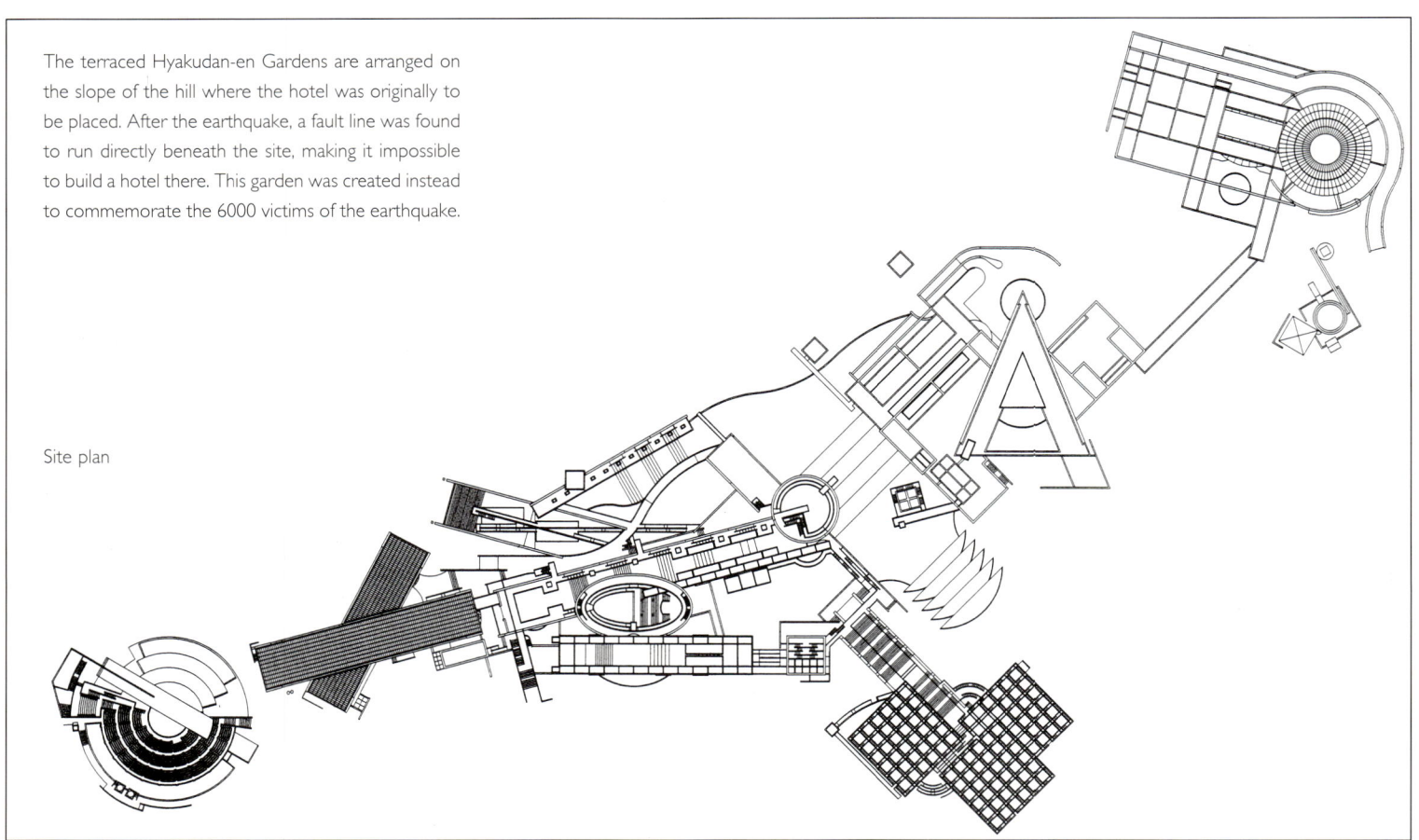

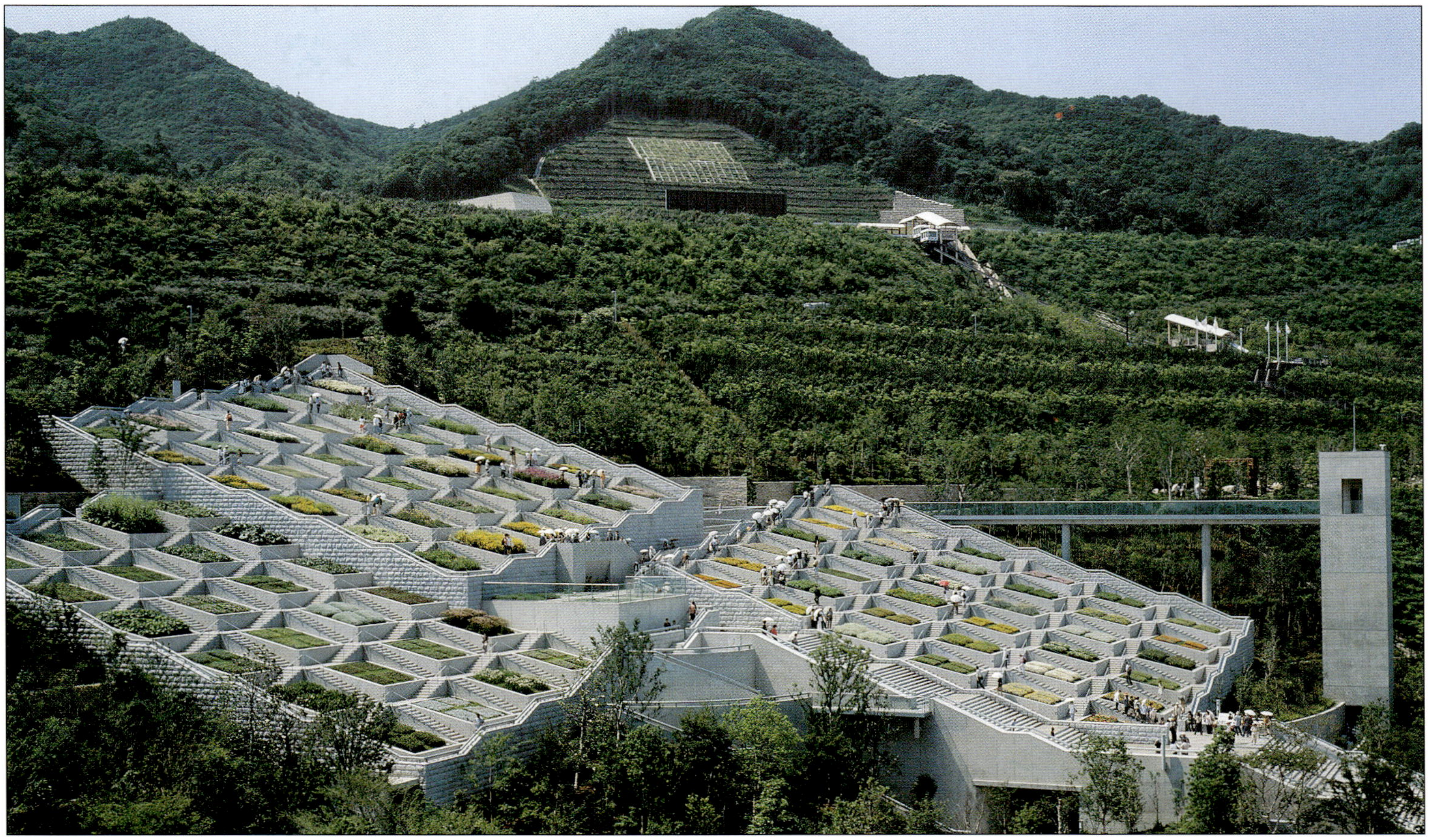

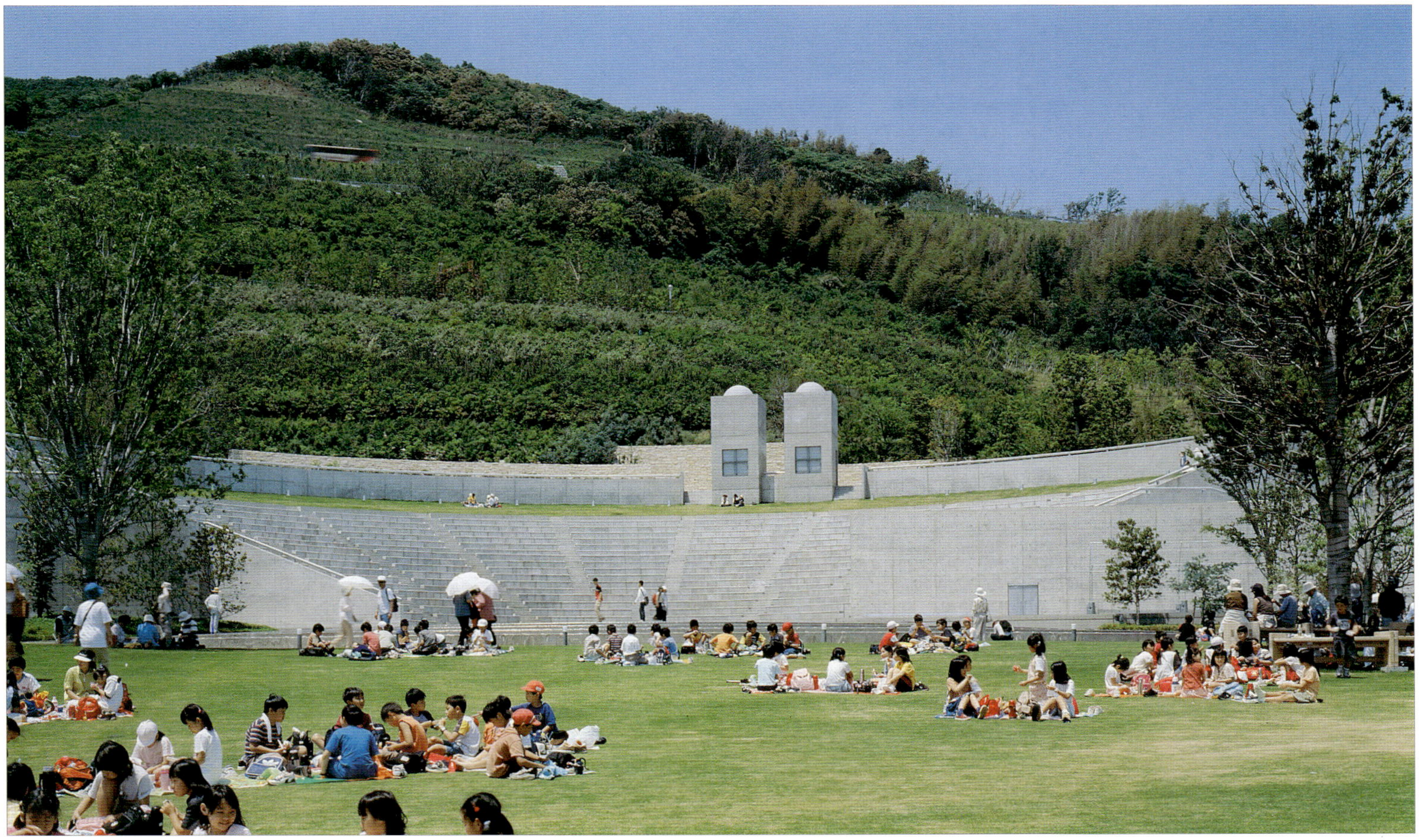

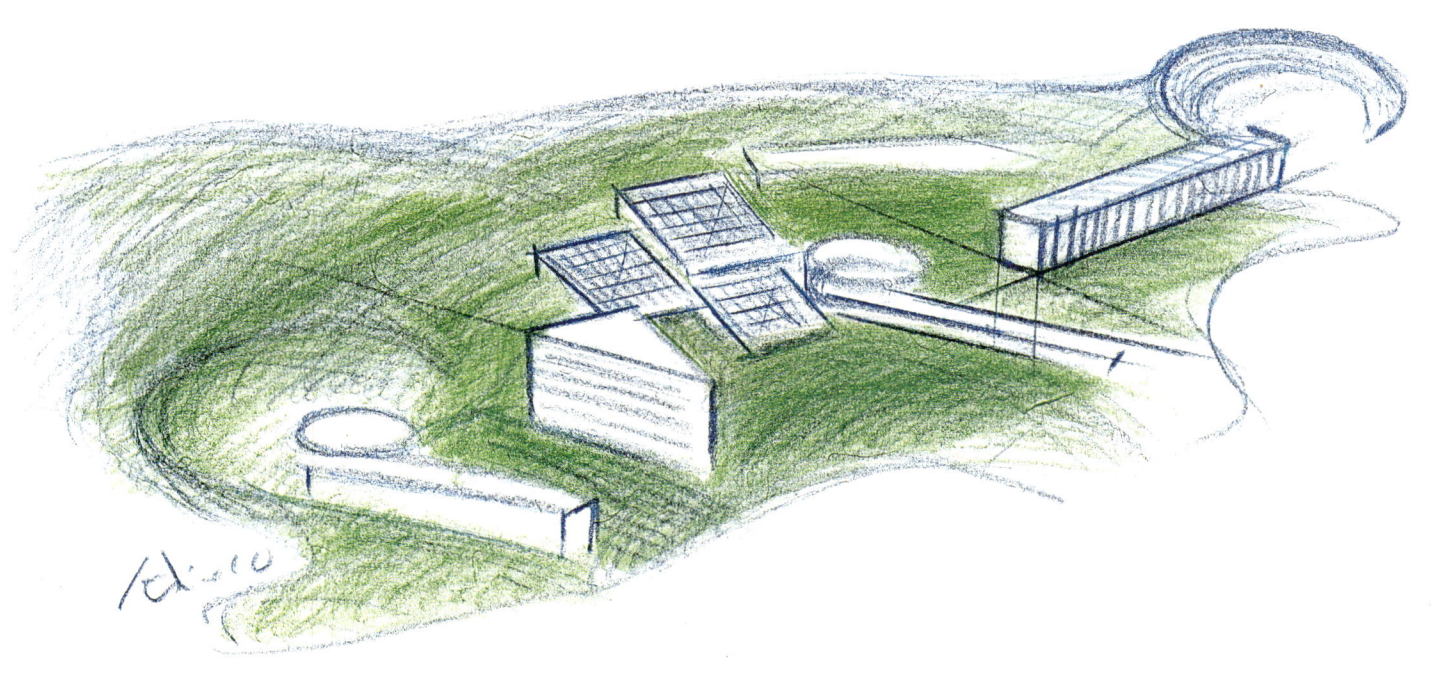

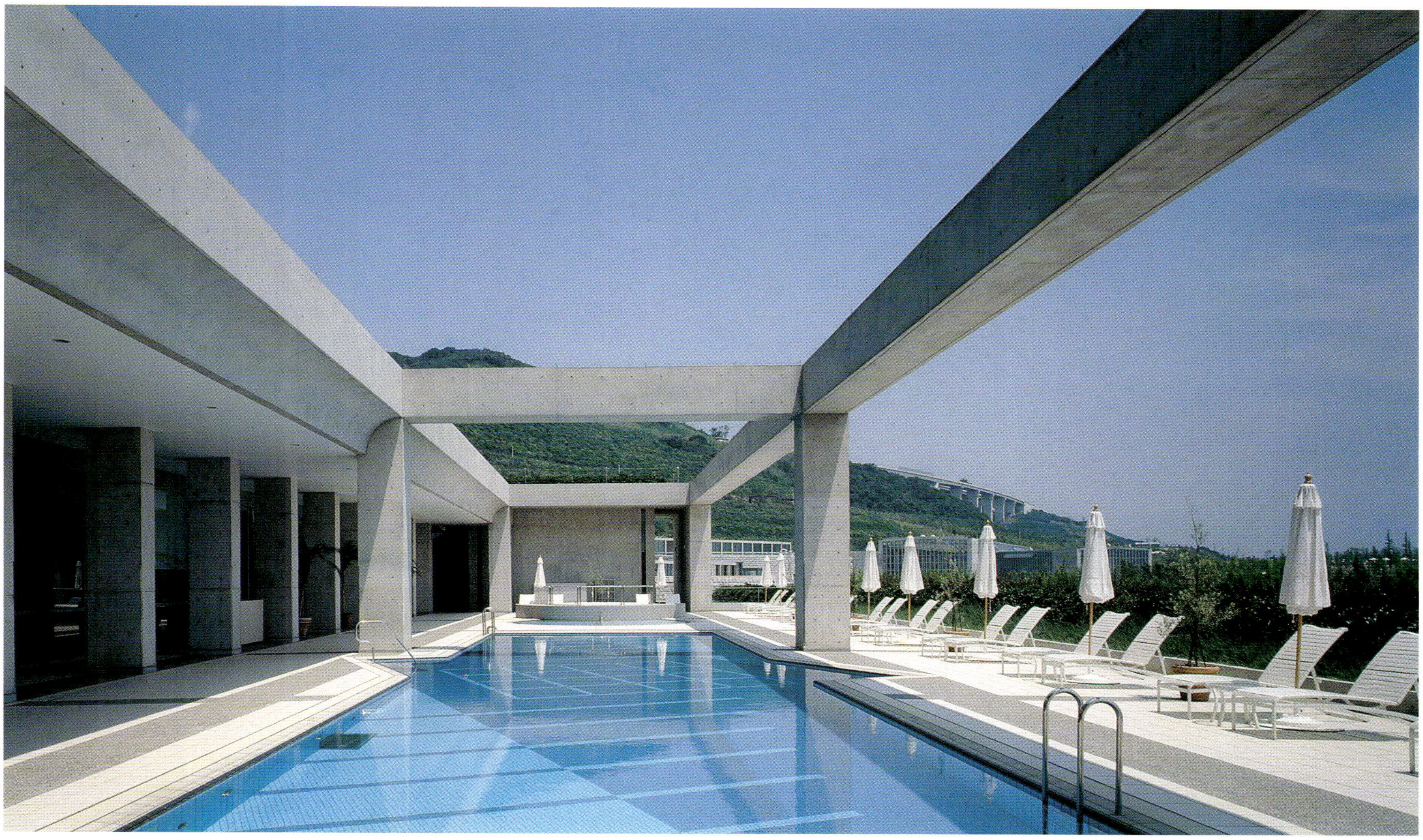

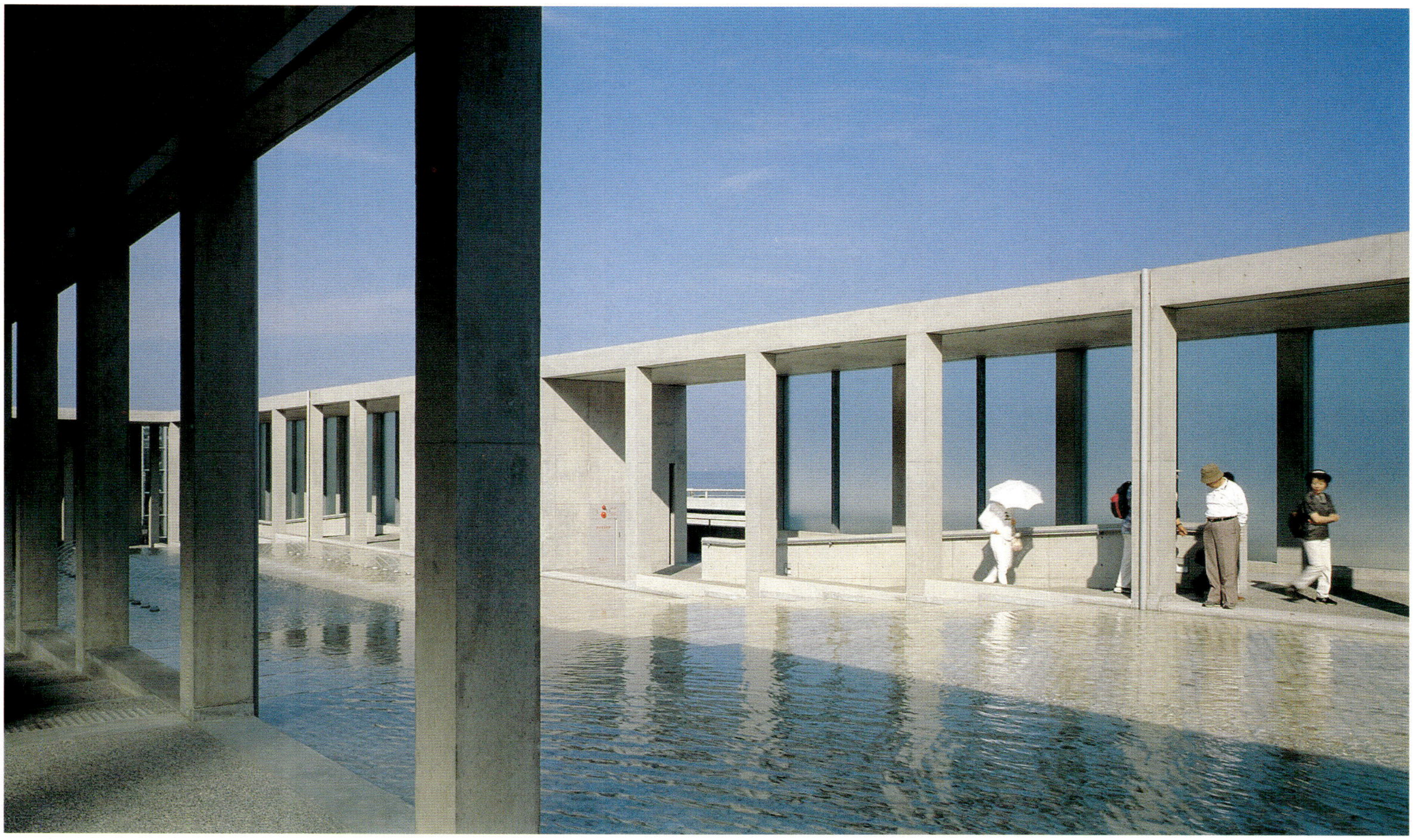

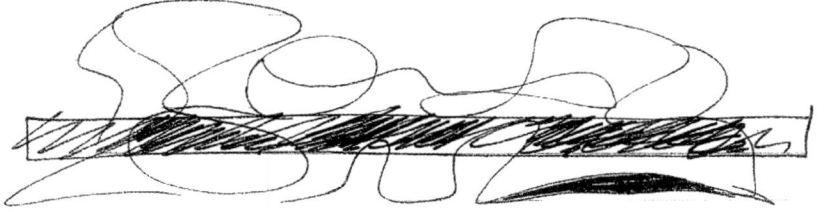

Zaha Hadid Architects
Phaeno Science Center Wolfsburg

Wolfsburg, Germany

Designed to present the visitor with a degree of complexity and strangeness ruled by a specific system the phaeno Science Centre awakens curiosity and discovery.

The building is located along a row of culturally significant buildings by Aalto, Scharoun and Schweger; performing as an urban barrier along the Bahnhofsstrasse, it encloses the northern edge of the inner city, while it simultaneously links into the new Volkswagen Autostadt.

The inner city's multiple lines of movement continue through the building at ground level. The axis of Wolfsburg's significant buildings enters the Science Center like a view through a kaleidoscope, and scatter towards the Volkswagen Autostadt.

The large space is supported and distributed by funnel-shaped cones, some of which give access to the space, others flood the inside with natural light, and still others house the service functions. The conical forms derive from the surrounding urban axis. These directions organically shape the building and its functions. One funnel becomes the main entrance, another becomes the lecture hall, and three more fuse into a big exhibition space under the main meeting hall: an alien, but oddly coherent crater landscape is the result.

The choice of materials continues the strategy of strangeness and fusion, based on the aesthetic effect of smooth, porous, sound-absorbing materials and different surface treatments.

Lighting used as an architectural asset establishes visual landmarks and allows for flexibility when charging exhibitions.

Exhibition designers can identify the "hidden pattern" of the service grid easily when installing a new show. The ceiling is simplified and a coherently organized service system allows vast open spaces as well as the installation of temporary walls. Light and shadow are the visual guidelines through the building, creating focal points and paths of light. The overall interior brightness requires to be tempered, to contrast with the highlighted exhibits. Visitors will intuitively follow the path of illuminated focal points. A smooth carpet of light provided underneath the building reflects light onto the underside of the sculptural forms. Increased illumination draws visitors to the entrances. The flow of visitors will determine other technical lighting requirements, including the creation of different zones.

Photographs: Michael Rasche / Artur, Roland Halbe / Artur,
Werner Huthmacher / Artur

© Roland Halbe / Artur

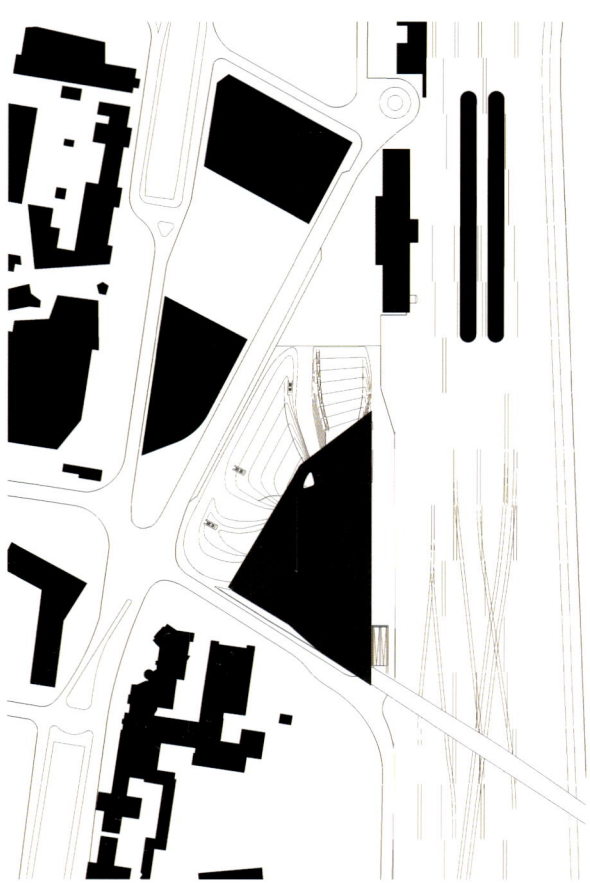

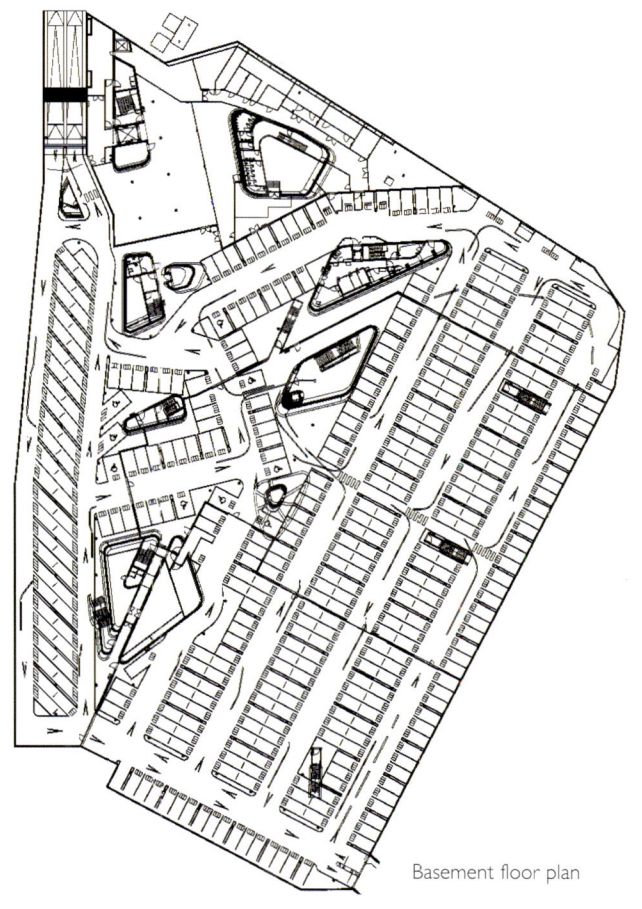

Basement floor plan

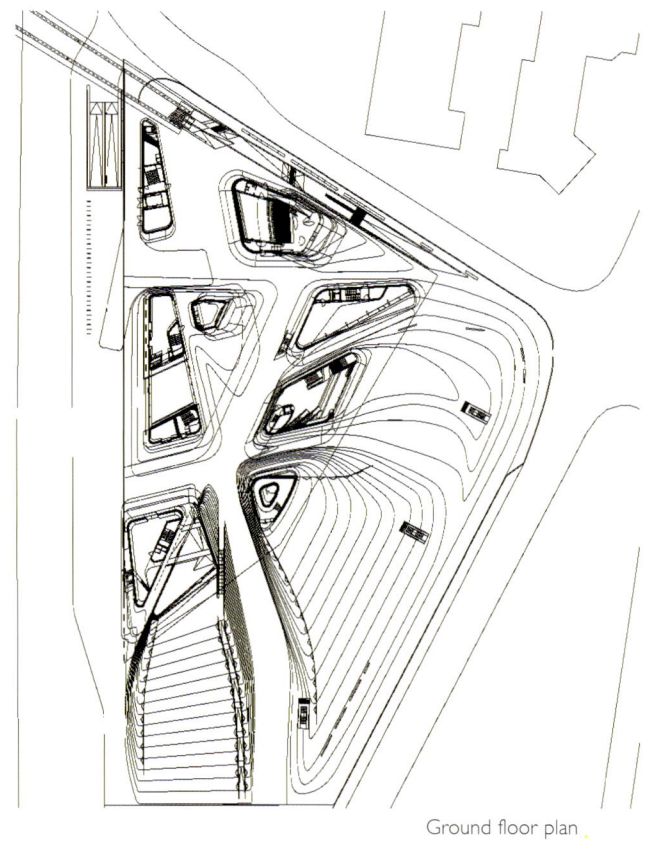

Ground floor plan

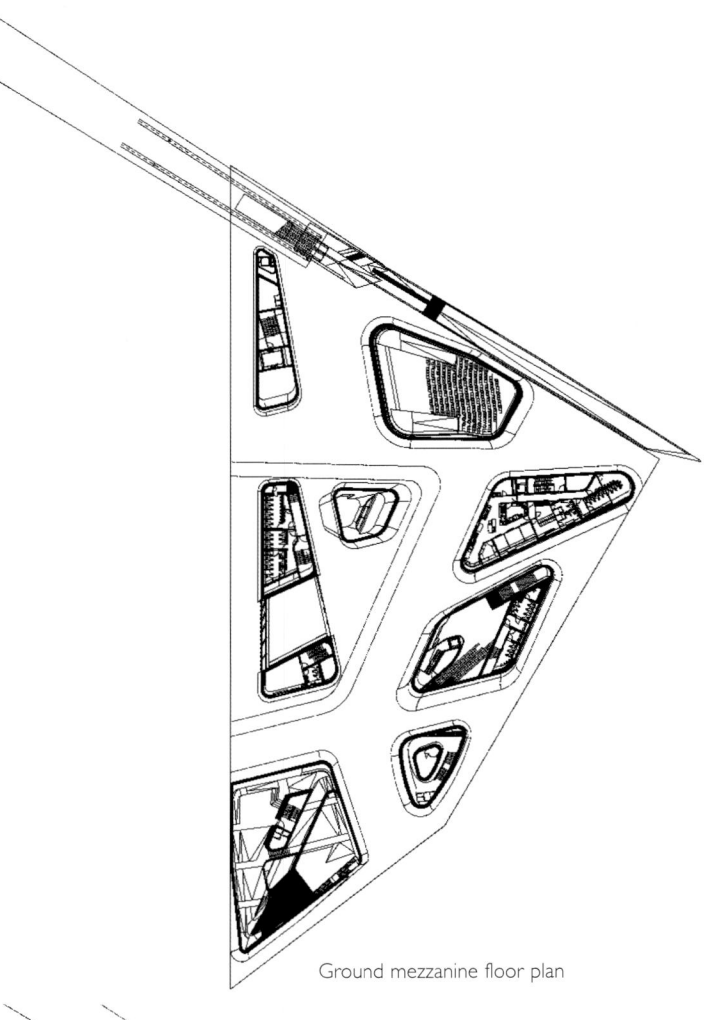

Ground mezzanine floor plan

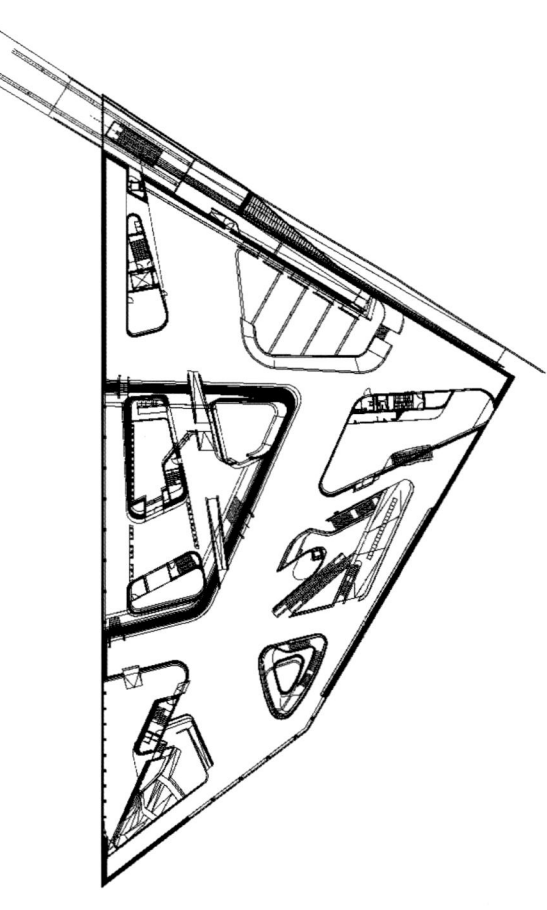

Concourse floor plan

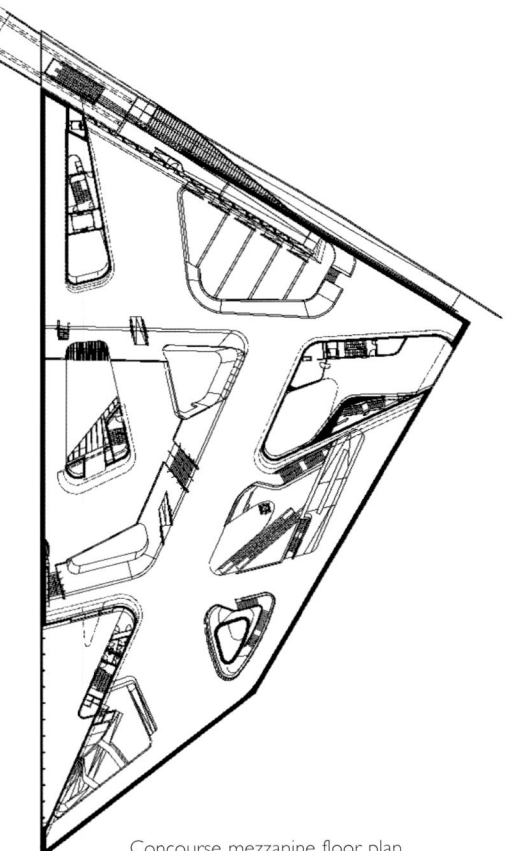

Concourse mezzanine floor plan

The conical forms derive from the surrounding urban axis. These directions organically shape the building and its functions. One funnel becomes the main entrance, another becomes the lecture hall, and three more fuse into a big exhibition space under the main meeting hall: an alien, but oddly coherent crater landscape is the result.

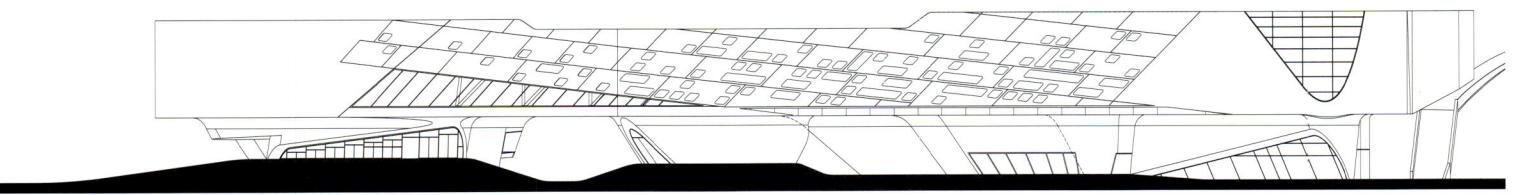

Elevation South

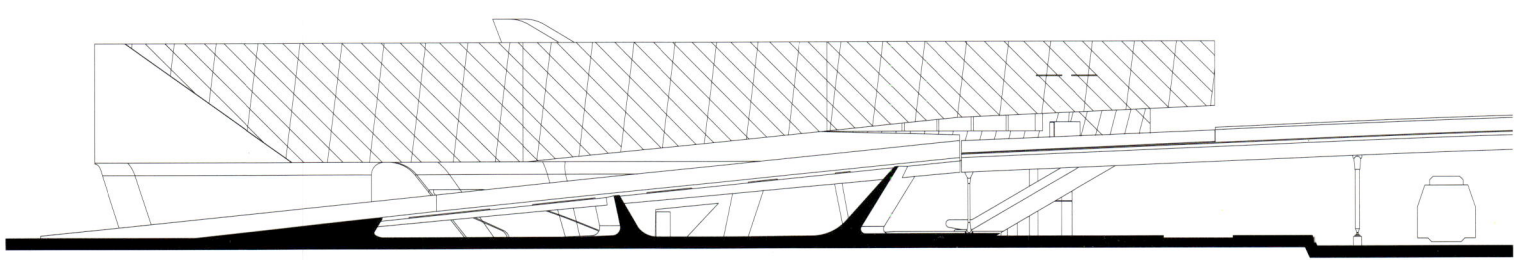

Elevation East

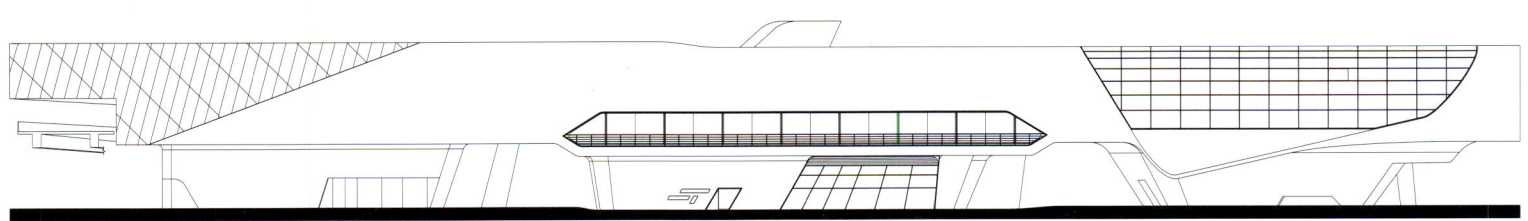

Elevation North

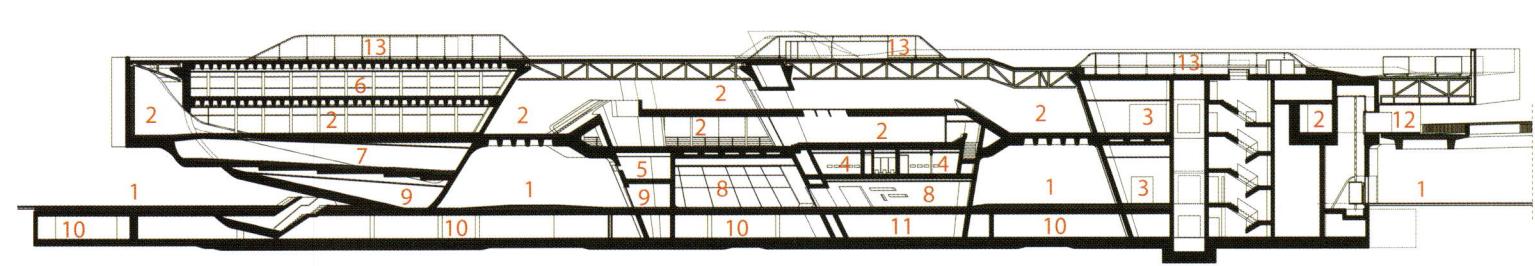

Section

1. Landscape
2. Exhibition room
3. Laboratory
4 Toilets
5 Staff room
6. Administration
7. Shop
8. Event space
9. Workshop
10. Parking
11. Toilets / Plant room
12. Bridge to autostadt
13. Plant room

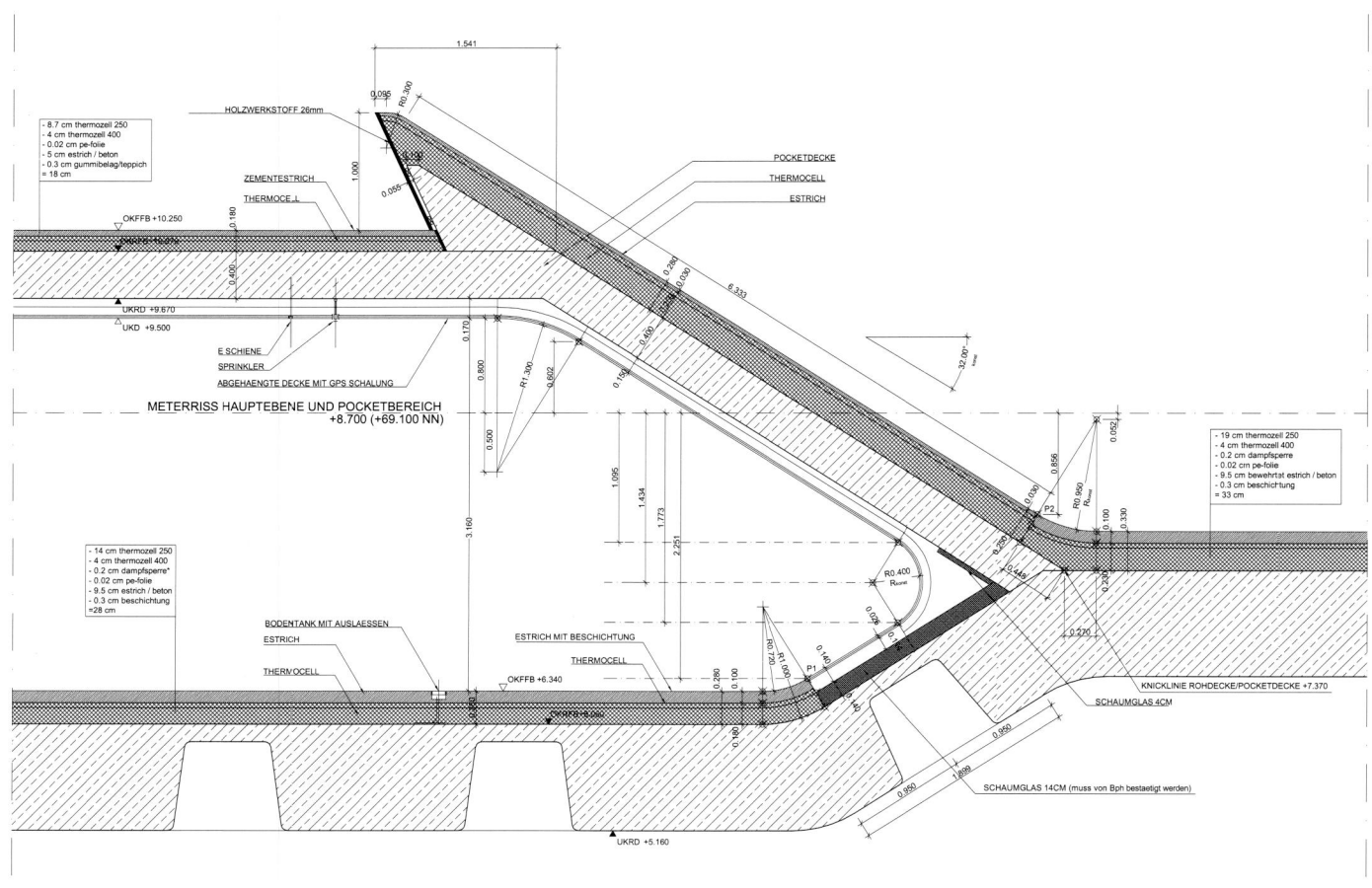

- 8.7 cm thermozell 250
- 4 cm thermozell 400
- 0.02 cm pe-folie
- 5 cm estrich / beton
- 0.3 cm gummibelag/teppich
= 18 cm

HOLZWERKSTOFF 26mm

POCKETDECKE

THERMOCELL

ESTRICH

ZEMENTESTRICH

THERMOCELL

OKFFB +10.250

UKRD +9.670

UKD +9.500

E SCHIENE

SPRINKLER

ABGEHAENGTE DECKE MIT GPS SCHALUNG

METERRISS HAUPTEBENE UND POCKETBEREICH
+8.700 (+69.100 NN)

- 19 cm thermozell 250
- 4 cm thermozell 400
- 0.2 cm dampfsperre
- 0.02 cm pe-folie
- 9.5 cm bewehrtst estrich / beton
- 0.3 cm beschichtung
= 33 cm

- 14 cm thermozell 250
- 4 cm thermozell 400
- 0.2 cm dampfsperre*
- 0.02 cm pe-folie
- 9.5 cm estrich / beton
- 0.3 cm beschichtung
=28 cm

BODENTANK MIT AUSLAESSEN

ESTRICH

THERMOCELL

OKFFB +6.340

ESTRICH MIT BESCHICHTUNG

THERMOCELL

KNICKLINIE ROHDECKE/POCKETDECKE +7.370

SCHAUMGLAS 4CM

SCHAUMGLAS 14CM (muss von Bph bestaetigt werden)

UKRD +5.160

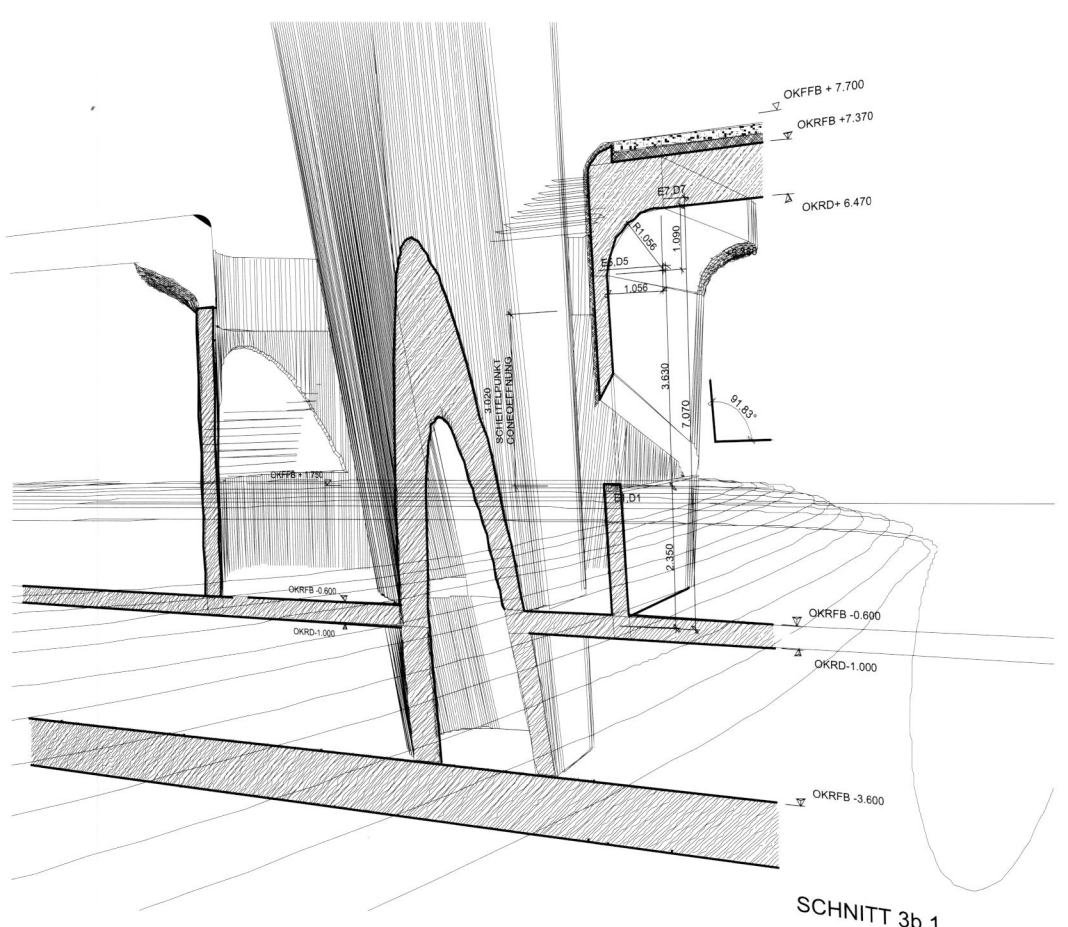

OKFFB + 7.700

OKRFB +7.370

OKRD+ 6.470

OKFFB + 1.750

OKRFB -0.600

OKRD-1.000

OKRFB -0.600

OKRD-1.000

OKRFB -3.600

SCHNITT 3b.1

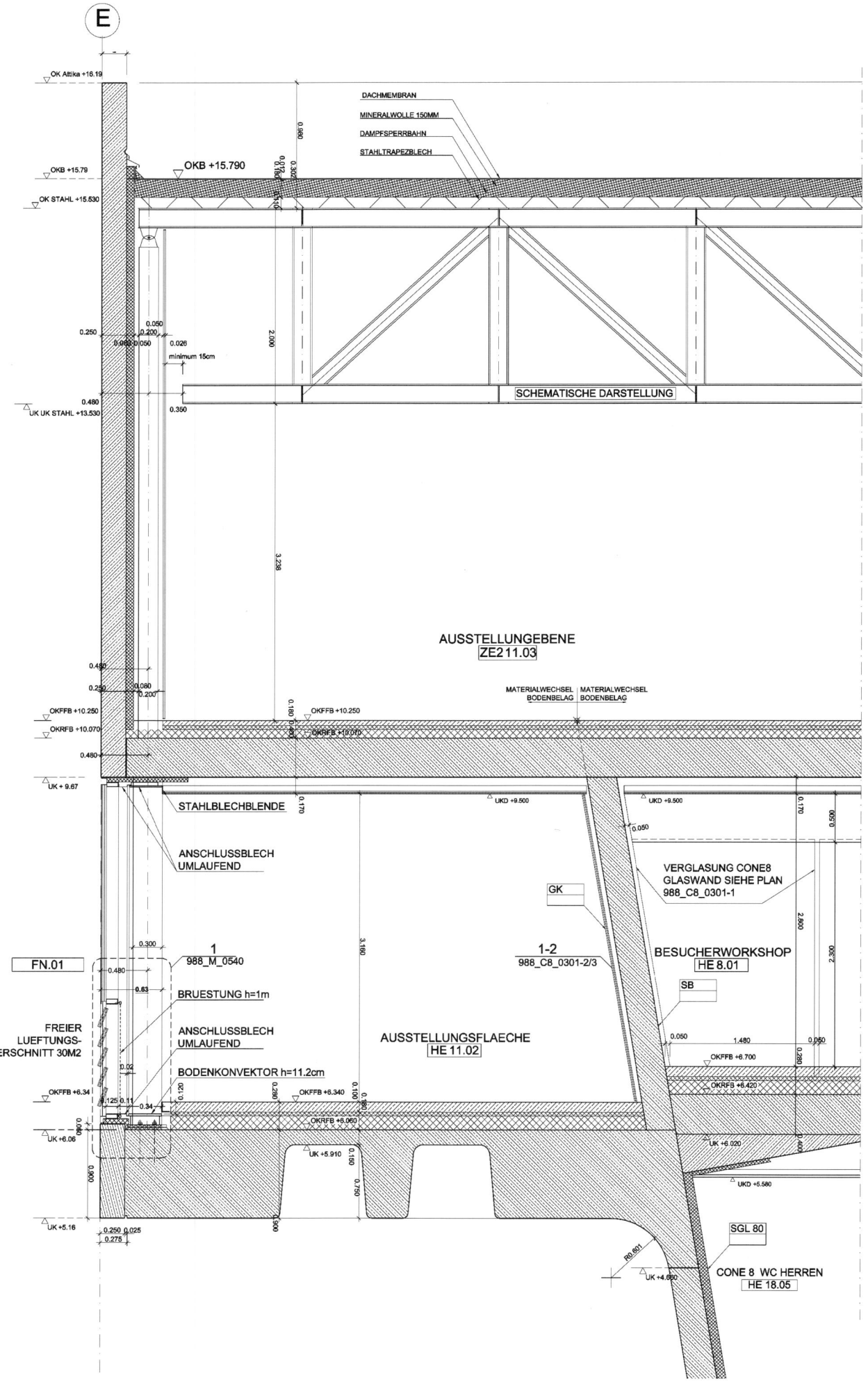

E

OK Attika +16.19

DACHMEMBRAN
MINERALWOLLE 150MM
DAMPFSPERRBAHN
STAHLTRAPEZBLECH

OKB +15.79   OKB +15.790

OK STAHL +15.530

0.900
0.302

0.250   0.050
             0.200
0.980 0.050   0.026
          minimum 15cm

2.000

UK UK STAHL +13.530   0.480
                      0.350

SCHEMATISCHE DARSTELLUNG

3.236

AUSSTELLUNGEBENE
ZE211.03

0.480   MATERIALWECHSEL | MATERIALWECHSEL
                   BODENBELAG | BODENBELAG
0.250   0.080
         0.200

OKFFB +10.250   OKFFB +10.250
OKRFB +10.070   OKRFB +10.070

0.480

UK + 9.67

STAHLBLECHBLENDE   UKD +9.500   UKD +9.500
                                            0.050

ANSCHLUSSBLECH
UMLAUFEND   VERGLASUNG CONE8
                                            GLASWAND SIEHE PLAN
                          GK   988_C8_0301-1

FN.01   1   1-2   BESUCHERWORKSHOP
          0.300   988_M_0540   988_C8_0301-2/3   HE 8.01
          0.480
          0.63   BRUESTUNG h=1m   SB

FREIER   ANSCHLUSSBLECH
LUEFTUNGS-   UMLAUFEND   AUSSTELLUNGSFLAECHE   1.480
QUERSCHNITT 30M2   HE 11.02
          0.02   OKFFB +6.700
          BODENKONVEKTOR h=11.2cm   OKRFB +6.420
OKFFB +6.34 0.120
          0.125 0.34   OKFFB +6.340
UK +6.06   OKRFB +6.060   UK +6.020
                  UK +5.910
                          0.750   UKD +5.580

UK +5.16   SGL 80
          0.250 0.025   R0.601
          0.275   CONE 8 WC HERREN
                                             UK +4.890   HE 18.05

116

Josef Paul Kleihues
Museum für Gegenwart im Hamburger Bahnhof

Berlin, Germany

Built in 1845-47, the Hamburger Bahnhof is a typical product of industrial era aesthetics, combining late Neo-classical masonry and the iron skeleton of the platform hall. It was closed in 1884 and converted into a transport and engineering museum in 1904-06. It was severely damaged in the Second World War and subsequently restored, to house a museum of contemporary art.

An attempt was made by extending the former station and adding additional buildings, to establish a dialogue with the old building. The buildings, lining the Historical Hall (formerly the Platform Hall) were replaced by two elongated barrel-vaulted galleries, united by the restored Central Hall with its iron and steel structure finished in grey metallic paint. The remainder of the masonry was a pattern of beams and columns. Externally, the existing ashlar masonry was finished in cream paint, which unifies the various parts. The Historical Hall received minimum interference, and reveals the order and rational geometry of the original structures. The two new gallery spaces have a steel-framed buttress structure filled in with cast aluminum panels or glass, contained within a limestone plinth and gables, and capped with a continuous glass roof over a barrel-vaulted ceiling.

The interiors of the galleries are very simple, with seamless floors laid with oak planks and white walls. Artificial lighting is either linear and is contained within the ceiling zone or in a universal gridded glass soffit.

With a variable top on side lighting system the Historical Hall can host huge exhibitions under the vaulted roof of the original railroad station.

Photographs: Hèléne Binet, Bildarchiv Preußischer Kulturbesitz, archive J.P. Kleihues

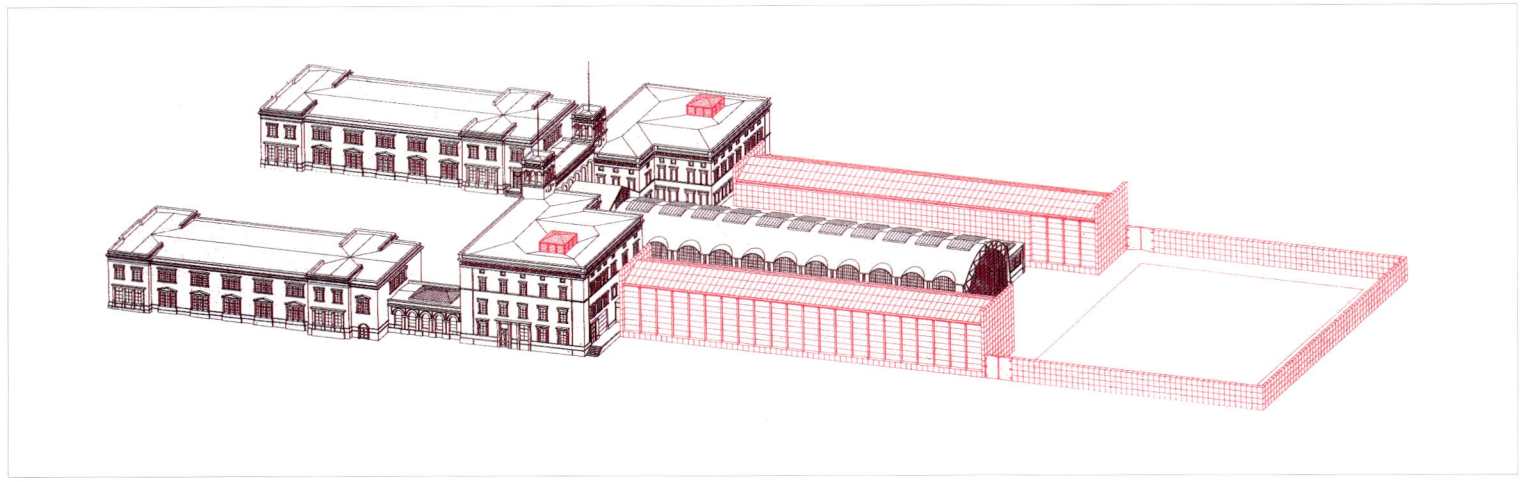

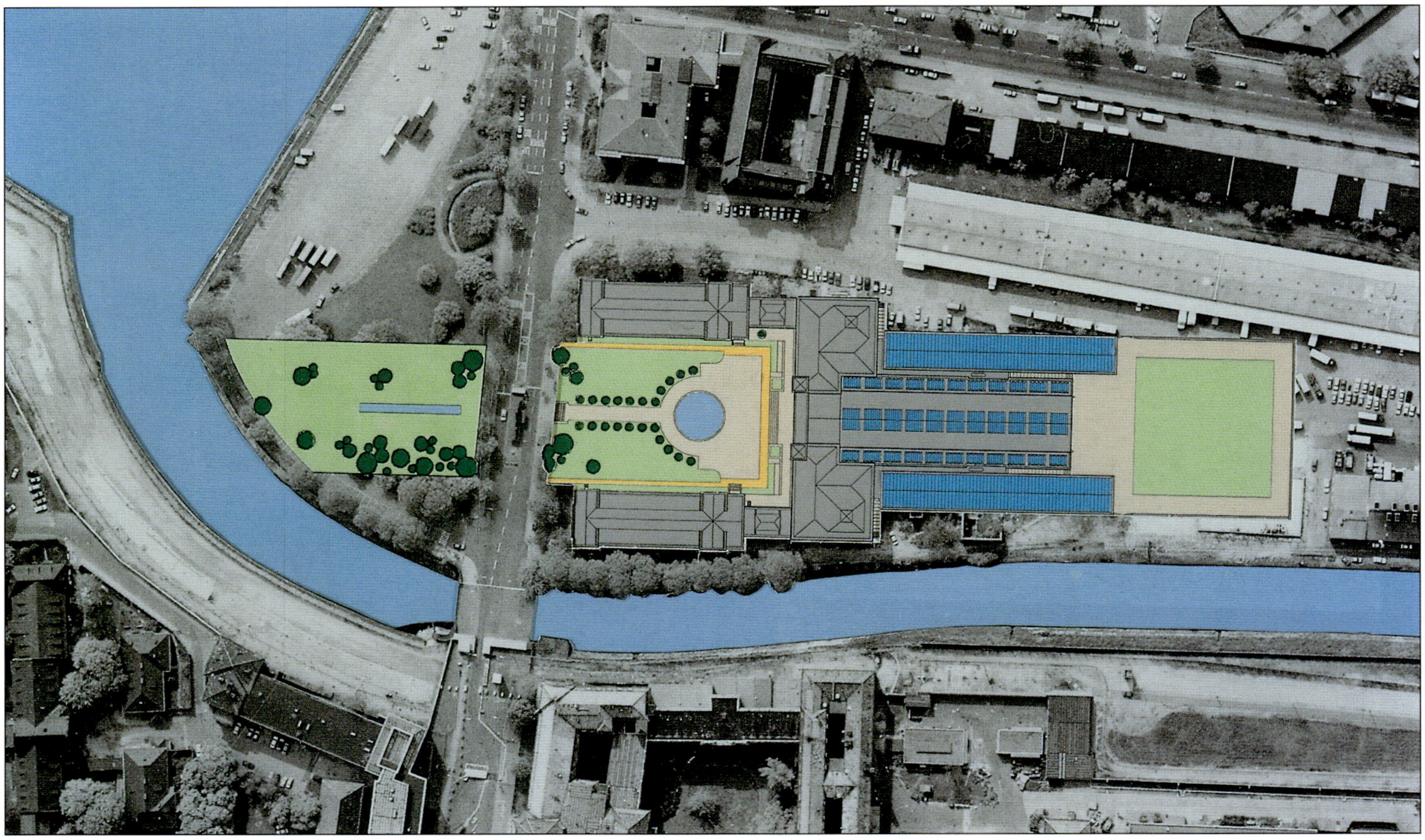

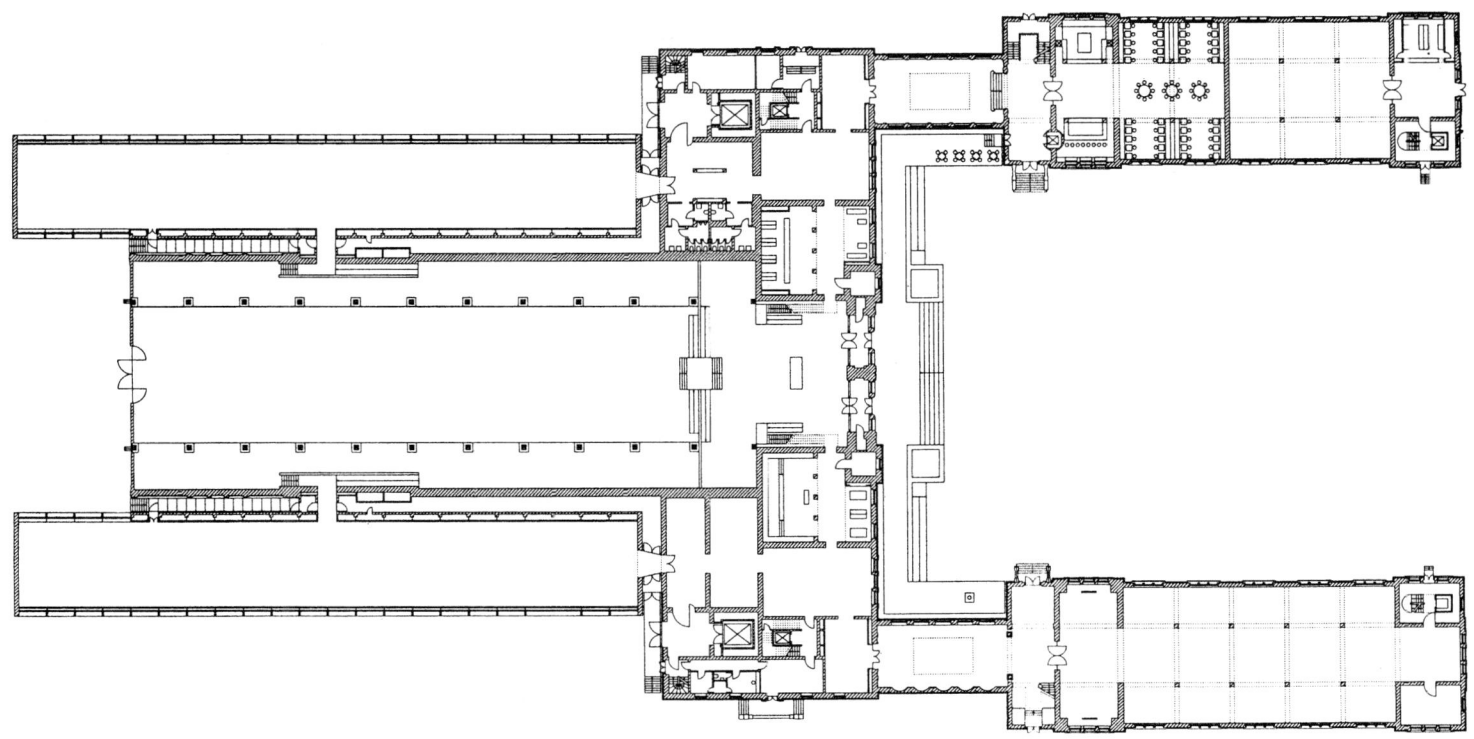

Upper floor plan

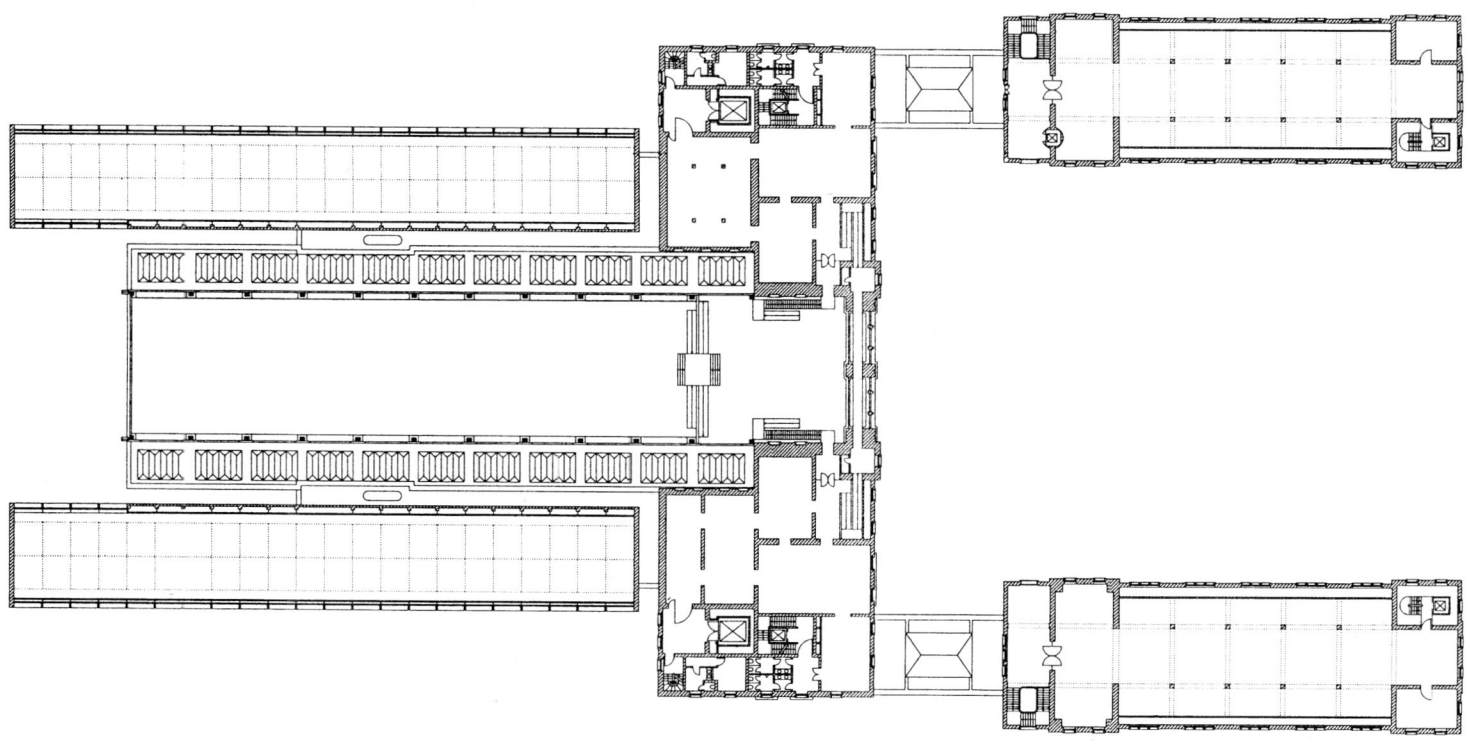

Ground floor plan

The galleries have been covered with a continuous glass roof over a barrel-vaulted ceiling.
The two new galleries have been built with a steel structure clad with cast aluminium panels or glass, according to the functional needs.

Through the conversión of the old station into a contemporay art museum and the addition of two new galleries, the project establishes a fluid dialogue between tradition and modernity.

William Bruder Architects
Deer Valley Rock Art Center

Phoenix, USA

The Deer Valley Rock Art Center represents a unique architectural solution featuring the sculptural use of precast concrete and weathering steel. The building is sited at the juncture of the two-mile-long earthen Adobe Mountain Dam and the Hedgpeth Hills formation. The building literally spans across the dam's flood control concrete outlet system. In so doing, the buildings´ geometry serves as a metaphorical "time machine" connecting the visitor between the chaos of suburban contemporary Phoenix and the sanctuary of the sheltered natural desert landscape of the Hedgpeth mountainside.

Beyond the uniqueness of the project's geometry and form is the originality of the exterior and interior exposed concrete finishes of the building. To complement and blend into the site, a coarse dark black/purple copper facing was placed in the casting beds of the precast panels and is naturally and completely adhered to the exterior faces. This combination of texture and colour was chosen as it blends perfectly into the black/purple color cast of the boulders of the mountain, making the structure almost invisible as it is approached from the east. Additionally, all panel joints disappear, except at the corners where the building's precast concrete nature is expressed by exposing the sandblasted grey edge thickness of the adjacent panels.

Photographs: Bill Timmerman

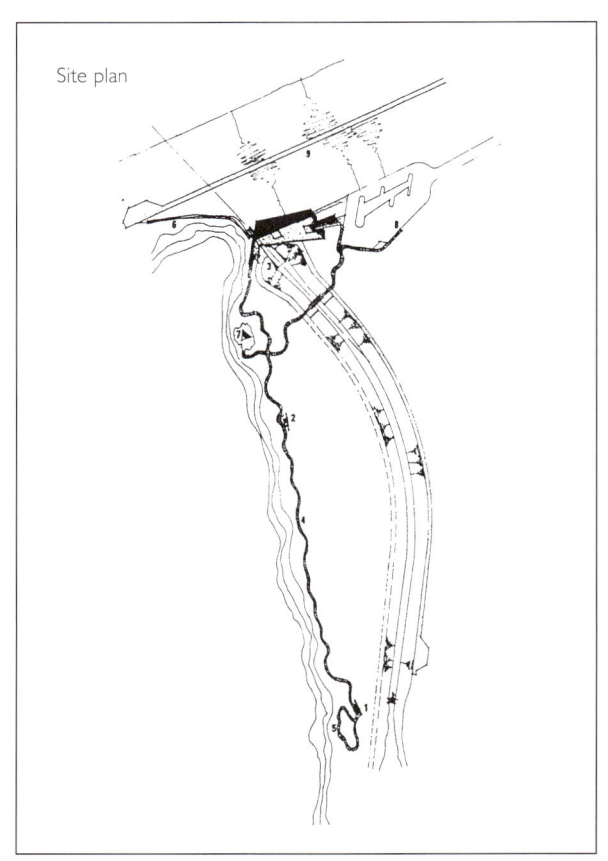

Site plan

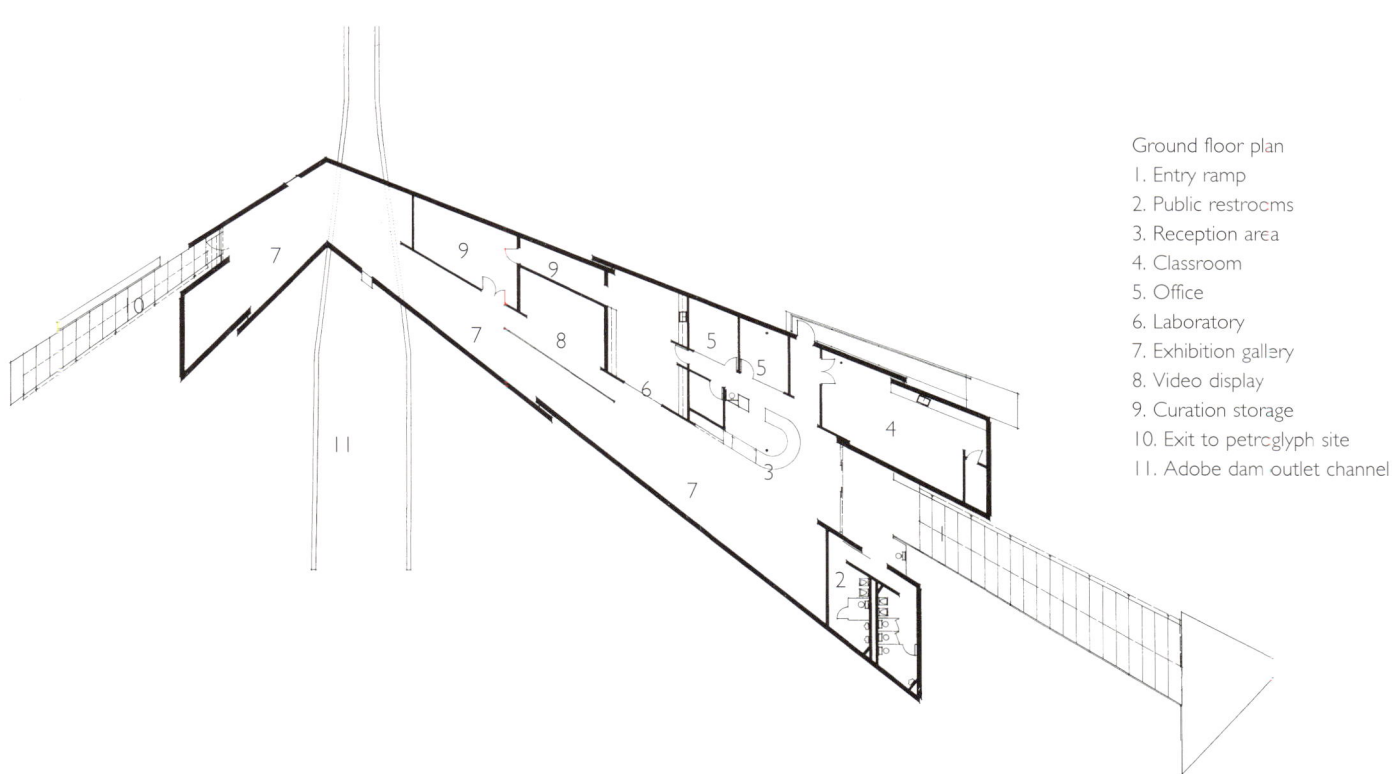

Ground floor plan
1. Entry ramp
2. Public restrooms
3. Reception area
4. Classroom
5. Office
6. Laboratory
7. Exhibition gallery
8. Video display
9. Curation storage
10. Exit to petroglyph site
11. Adobe dam outlet channel

The building was based on a single architectural solution in which the sculptural use of reinforced concrete is dominant.

The textures and colours of the prefabricated exterior panels were chosen in order to achieve a perfect integration with the dark purple colour of the adjacent mountains.

The interior houses spaces for exhibitions, research, study rooms and materials storage rooms.

All the concrete interior walls were left exposed without treatment, and their texture is like that of fine plaster. The walls were also fitted with thermal insulation.

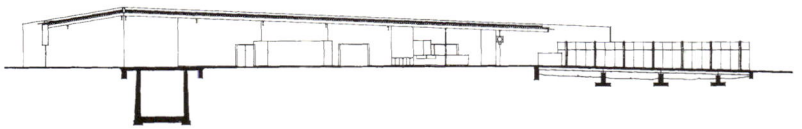

Longitudinal section

Paulo Mendes Da Rocha
Pinacoteca do Estado

São Paulo, Brazil

Although this late 19th century building, which was meant to house the Arts and Trades Lyceum, was never completed, it was kept in solid condition, with no cracks or foundational problems. Its underlying structure was also intact, although the delicate ornamental profiles sculpted from clay brick were highly deteriorated.

The project's primary goal was the technical adaptation of the building for housing the Pinacoteca do Estado (National Art Gallery). Its identity was defined by the urban location, its interior spaces and the potential public, as well as by the idea of expanding the property and the reception hall for temporary exhibits.

The program set out to solve the building's inherent problems: moisture, which was downgrading the thick walls; the complicated distribution of the exhibit areas scattered across several rooms and structured on the basis of interior voids formed by a central, octagonal rotunda and two rectangular side courtyards

The interior window frames were set back from the facade, thereby keeping the gaps open and generating high transparency, while highlighting the thick load-bearing brick walls.

The original construction was respected and the imprints of the old scaffolding, construction work and previous uses were conserved. The exterior facades were preserved by the cleaning and neutralizing of accumulated harmful deposits. The countless meandering paths of aged sculpted brick ornaments were kept intact, while chemically protecting them to conserve their color and texture.

As the primary material used in the renovation, steel has been used on the raised walkways, elevators and new stairways, in the structures of the new floors and roofs and in the windows and false ceilings. Such use is justified by the adaptation of local working conditions, by its relative lightness and the desire to establish thought-provoking dialogue with the original structure - between the new and the old.

Collaborators: Eduardo Colonelli, Welinton Torres

Photographs: Nelson Kon

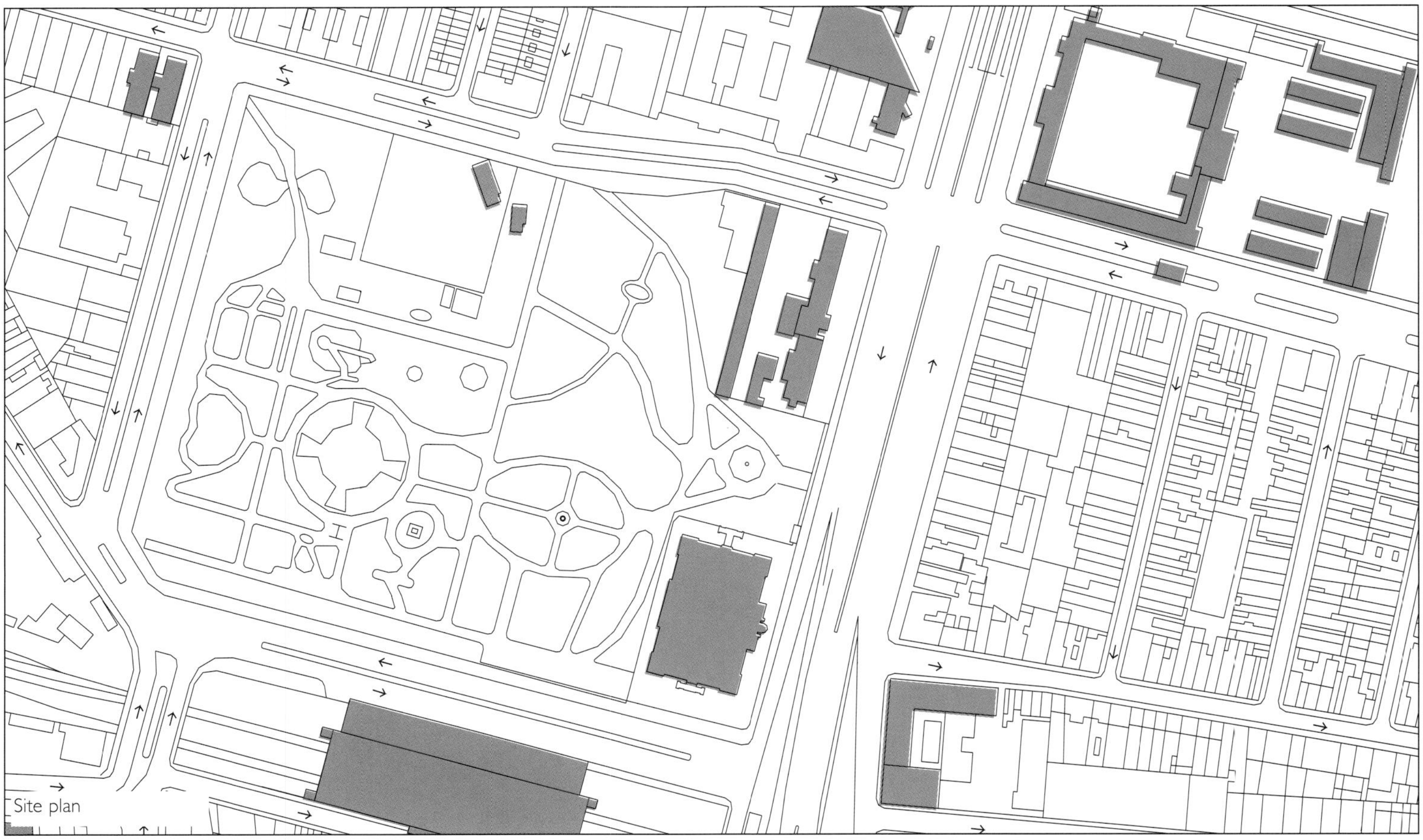

Site plan

137

Its urban location and the creation of new circulation routes along the building's longitudinal axis meant that the museum entrance could be placed in front of the Plaza de Luz, on the south face. This altered the relationship of the building to the city and called attention to the terraces as welcoming havens.

Flat skylights of steel profiles and glass laminate cover the interior voids, keeping rainwater out and ensuring the reproduction of the original lighting and ventilating conditions.

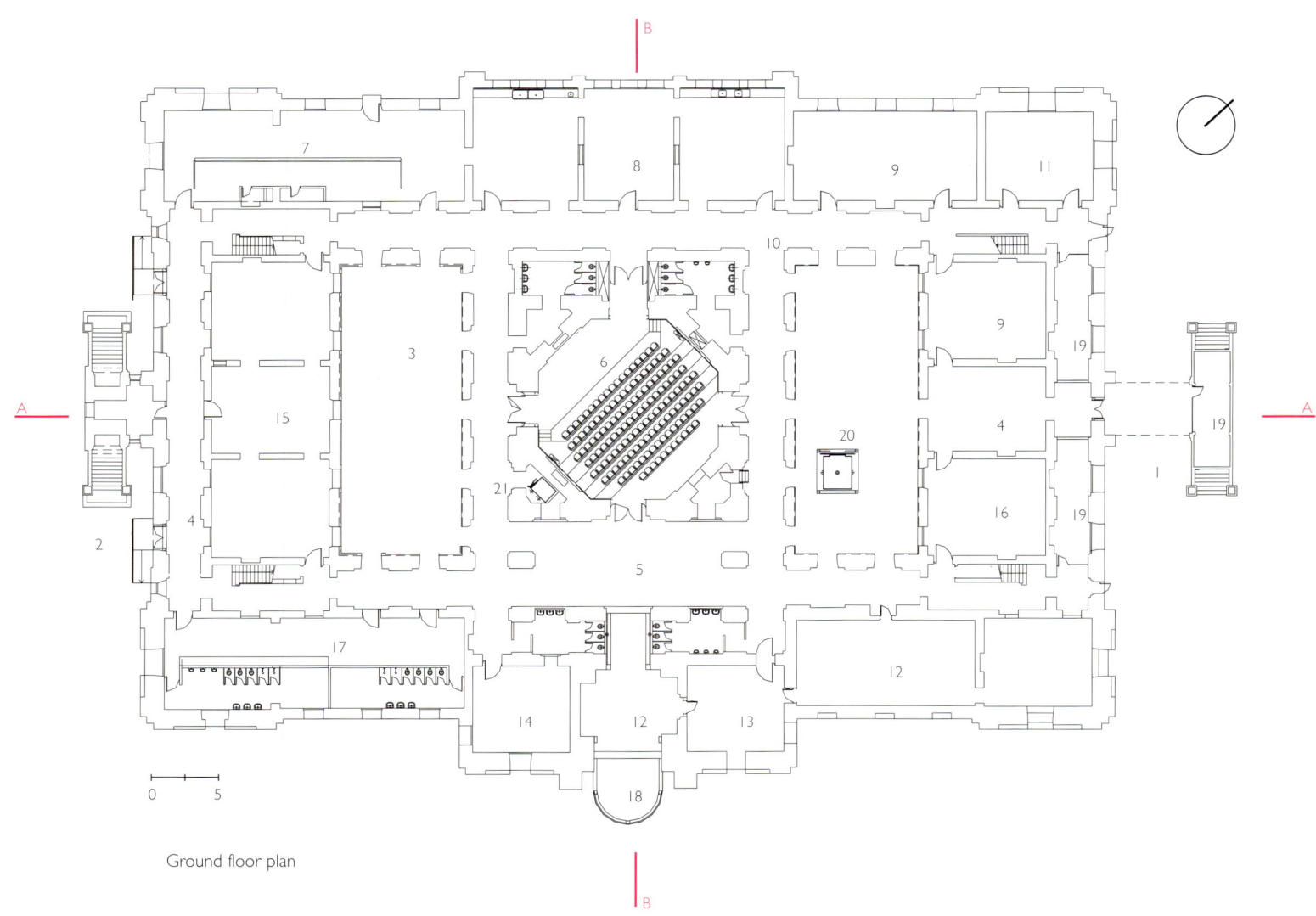

Ground floor plan

1. Services entrance
2. Public entrance
3. Courtyard
4. Porter's office
5. Foyer
6. Auditorium
7. Restaurant

8. Restoration lab
9. Montage
10. Gallery
11. Carpenter's shop
12. Artwork storage
13. Artwork restoration
14. Offices

15. Library
16. Temporary exhibit space
17. Staff dressing rooms
18. Machine room
19. Storage
20. Elevator

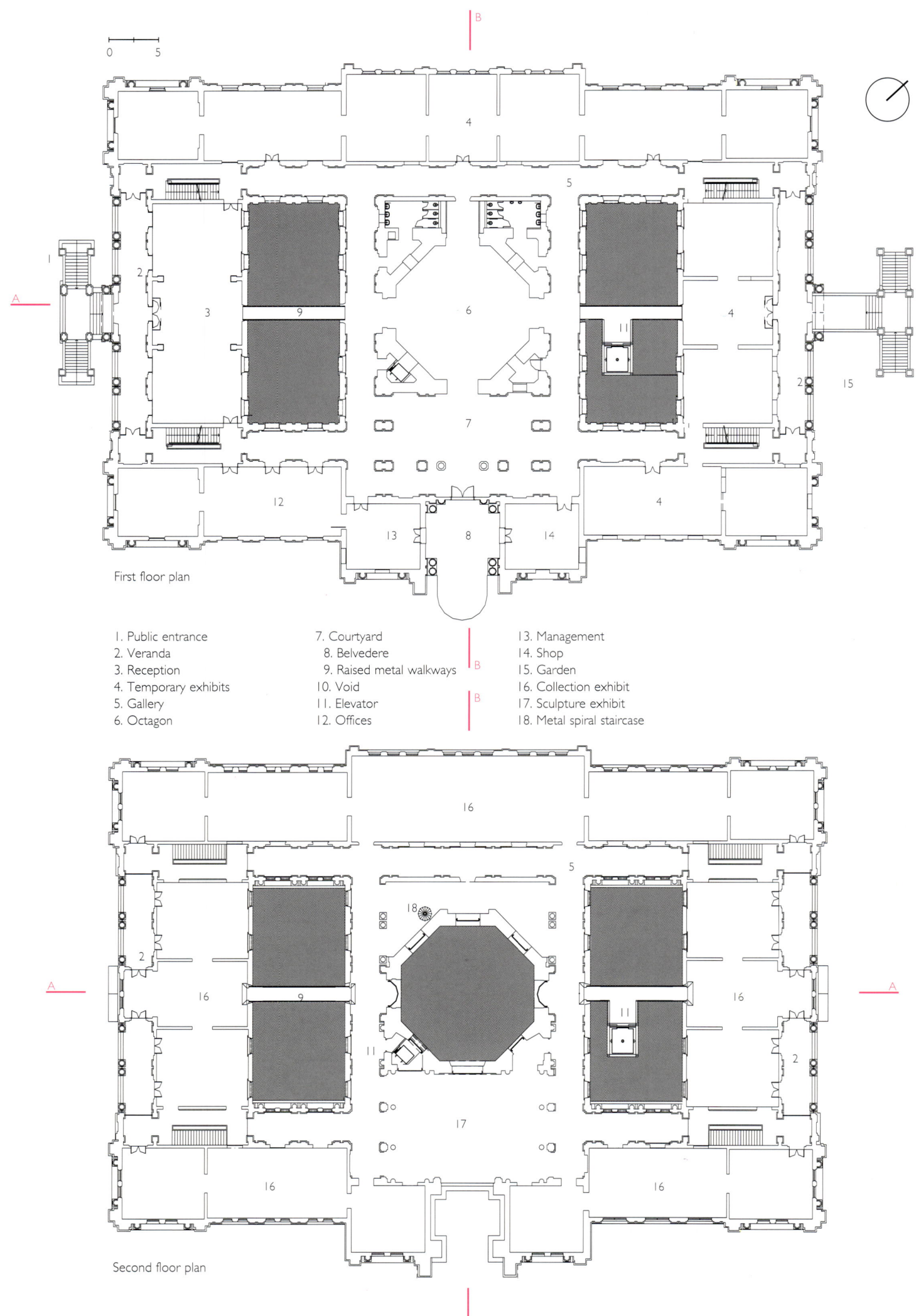

First floor plan

1. Public entrance
2. Veranda
3. Reception
4. Temporary exhibits
5. Gallery
6. Octagon

7. Courtyard
8. Belvedere
9. Raised metal walkways
10. Void
11. Elevator
12. Offices

13. Management
14. Shop
15. Garden
16. Collection exhibit
17. Sculpture exhibit
18. Metal spiral staircase

Second floor plan

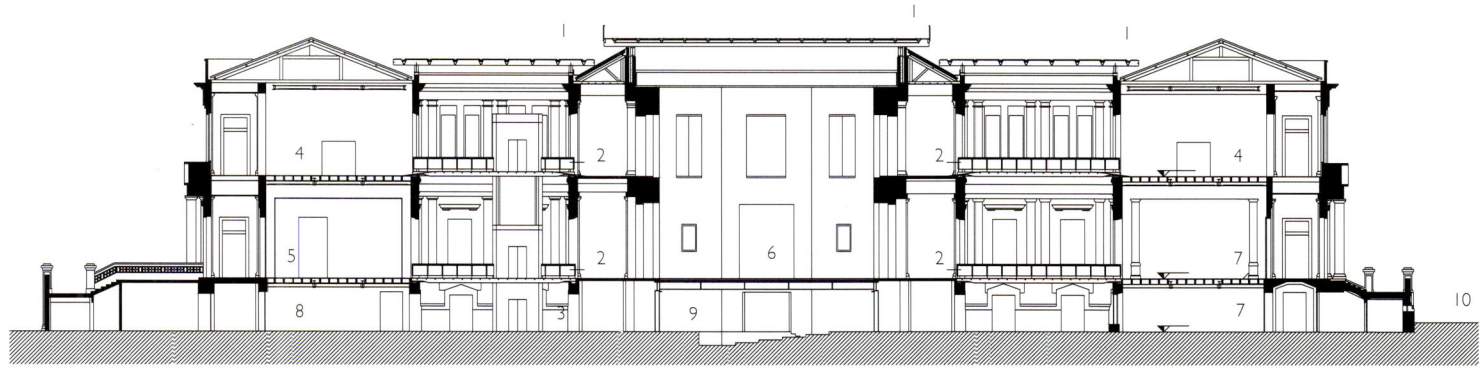

Section AA

1. Skylight
2. Raised metal walkway
3. Elevator shaft
4. Collection exhibit
5. Temporary exhibits
6. Octagon
7. Reception
8. Porter's office
9. Auditorium
10. Public entrance
11. Machine room-Water depositories
12. Belvedere
13. Restoration lab

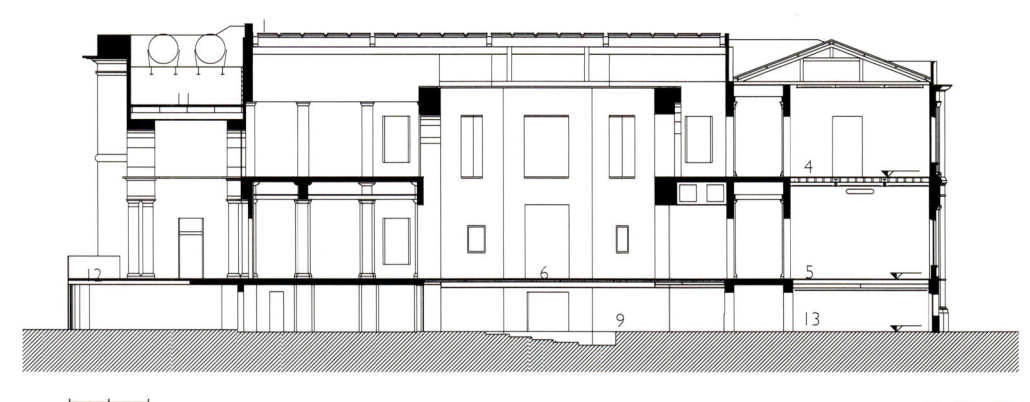

Section BB

0   5

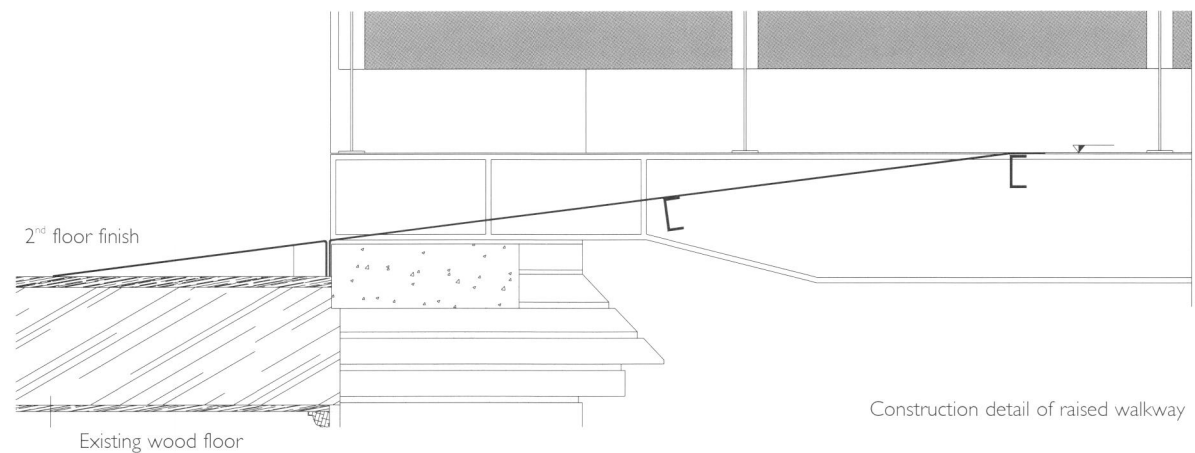

2nd floor finish

Existing wood floor

Construction detail of raised walkway

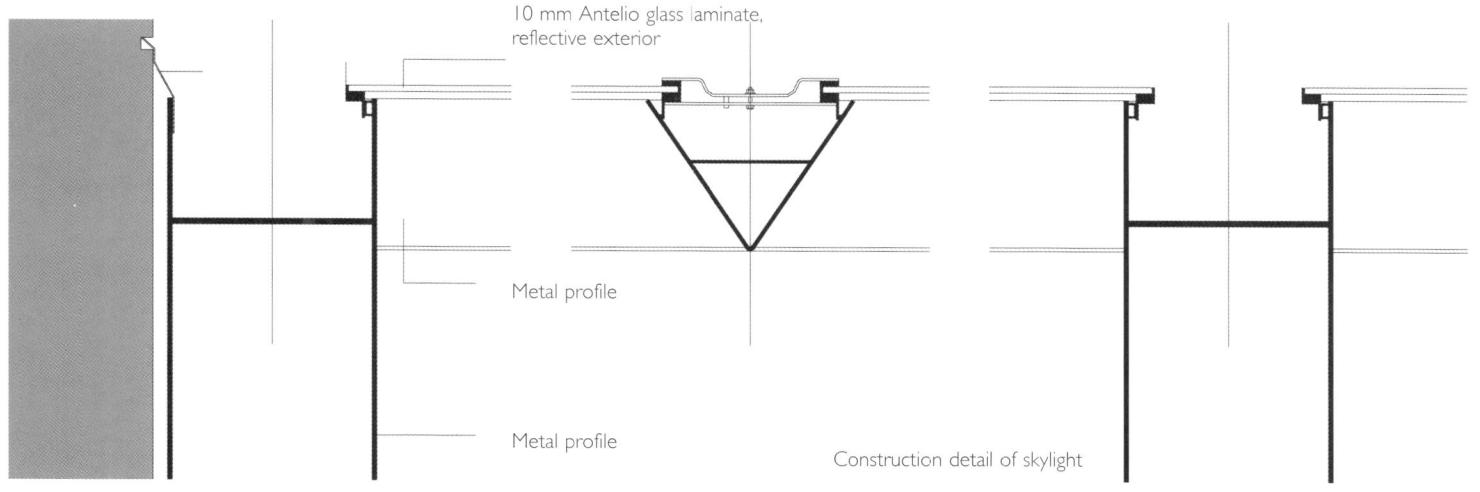

10 mm Antelio glass laminate, reflective exterior

Metal profile

Metal profile

Construction detail of skylight

143

Kisho Kurokawa & Associates
The Museum of Modern Art

Wakayama, Japan

The site is located on what used to be a part of the ancient Wakayama Castle grounds, and at present this area is divided into two with a road running in between. The other divided area would become a park and eventually be connected by a wide pedestrian walkway over the road.

Castle architecture in Japan was first developed in the fifteenth, sixteenth and seventeenth centuries. The design of the roof and the eaves symbolises this style.

The museum expresses the symbiosis of history and the present by using the traditional eaves but in an abstract way.

The colours proposed here are black and white, which is also taken from the traditional castle architecture style.

The art museum as well as the prefectural museum are designed with simple geometric forms. In addition to the crescent geometric interrelation, the exterior finish of the art museum is proposed in black ceramic tile, while the prefectural museum is proposed in white ceramic tile.

The arrangement of architecture and its forms are carefully designed to evade symmetry.

The edge of the pond, where the site is situated, is designed linearly, and the park side is designed with natural curves so as to express the traditional Japanese culture of asymmetry.

Photographs: Norihisa Ohnishi

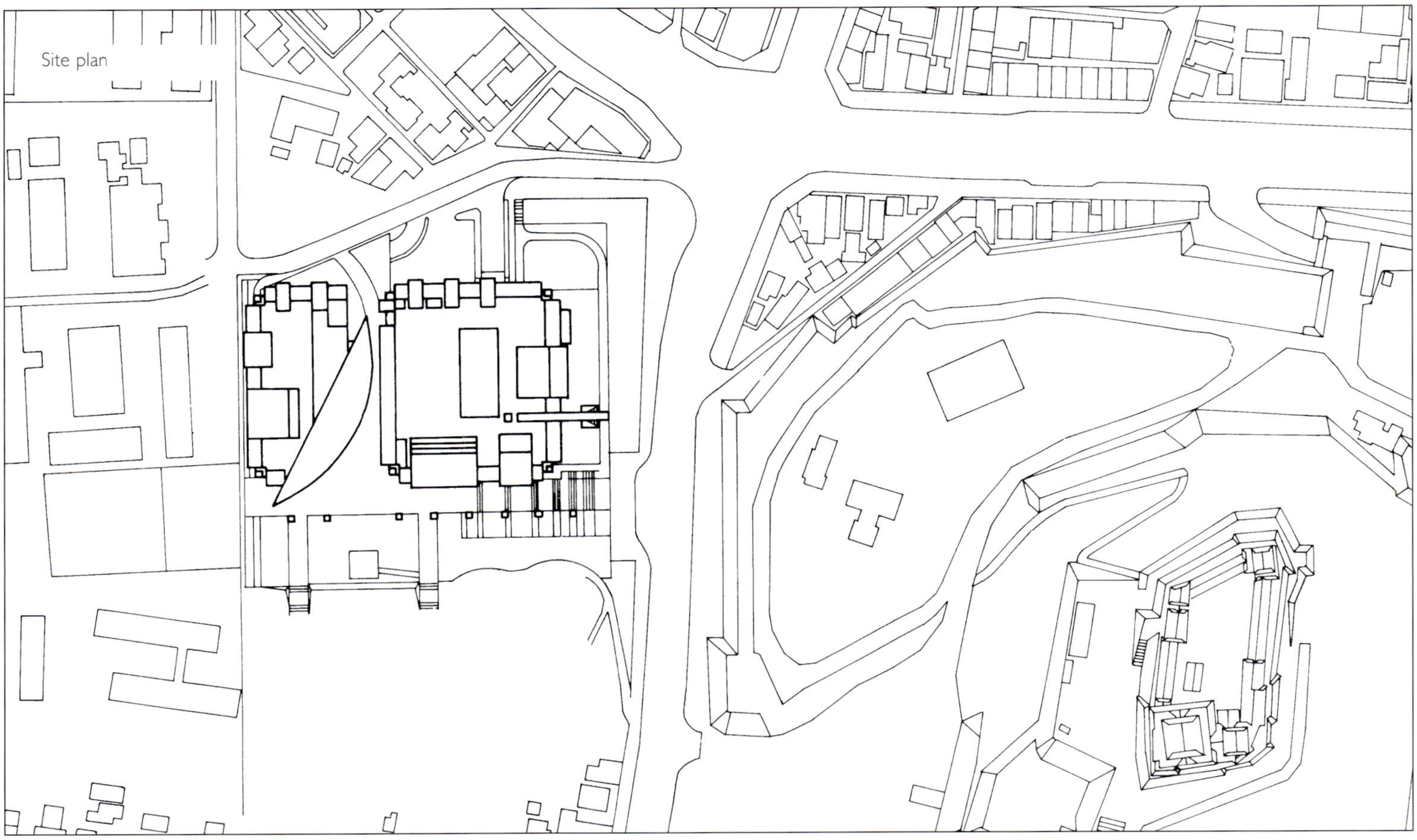

Site plan

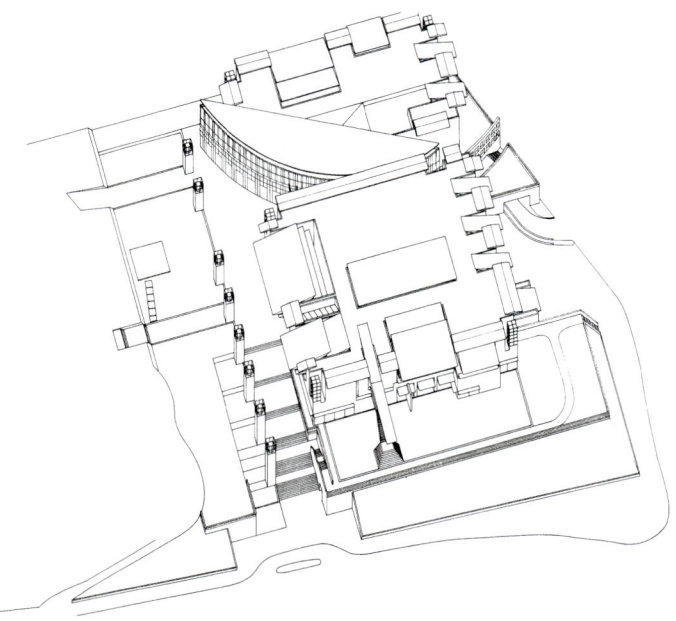

The new museum, situated on the land of the old Wakayama castle, is a construction of simple and expressive geometric forms that connects perfectly with the character of traditional Japanese architecture. Also, the architectural order, the building forms, the textures and even the colours were chosen expressly to avoid symmetry or the repetition of similar structures.

The eaves were based on traditional Japanese architecture, but are far more stylized.

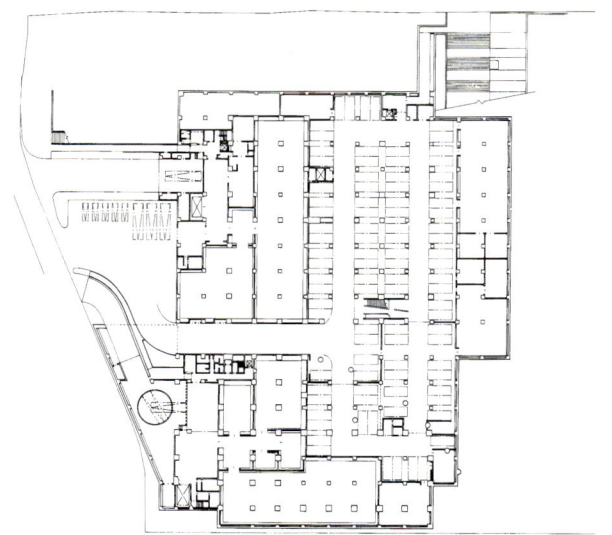

First basement floor plan

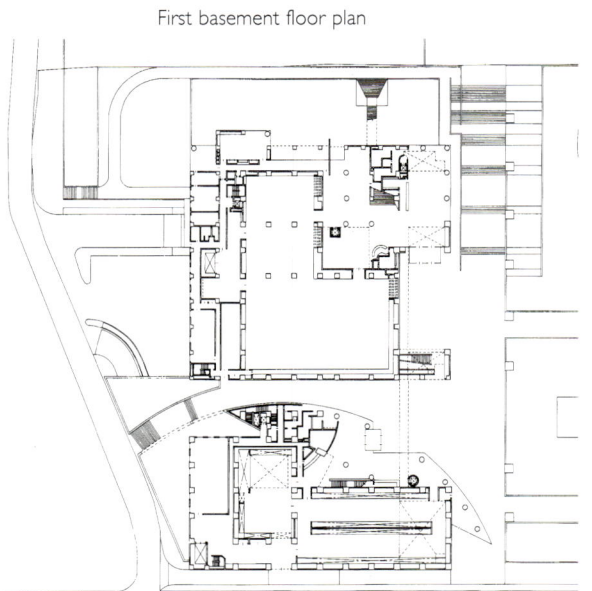

First floor plan

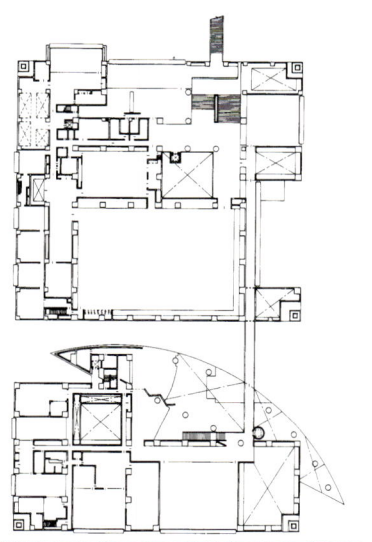

Second floor plan

Opaque partitions were avoided in the interior to make the spaces brighter and more diaphanous. The interior finishes of structures (staircases and pillars), furniture and fittings fit into a strict asymmetric order, which evokes certain aspects of traditional Japanese culture.

Mansilla + Tuñón Arquitectos
MUSAC in León

León, Spain

On an expanse of urban space, the MUSAC outlines a stage for art with the same optimistic attitude with which the Roman town-planners traced their cities on the landscape. Compared to other types of museum spaces, the characteristic of which is to house closed historical collections, the MUSAC is a living space that opens its doors to a variety of contemporary artistic manifestations; an art center that creates a series of playing boards and where the installations are the main actors of the space itself. A structure developed on an open plan system, consisting of a network of squares and rhomboids that allow a secret geography of memory to materialize.

The 10.000 m² of the MUSAC house a new space for culture, defining culture as that which helps to reveal the links between man and nature.

In this serial chain of autonomous halls, exhibitions of a different nature can be installed; the broken form of the various halls creates different spatial characteristics throughout the continuous space. Each hall opens into the other halls and courtyards, allowing longitudinal, transversal and diagonal vistas to appear. Five hundred prefabricated concrete beams bridge the spaces, whose main feature is systematic repetition and formal expressiveness.

The public space outside acquires a concave form, to host activities and meetings; enclosed by large colored sheets of glass, it pays homage to the city as the context of human encounters. Within it, a great area of continuous but alternative spaces, interspersed with courtyards and great skylights, contributes to create an expressive system that transmits the shared interests of architecture and art: the contemporary perception of what is variable and what is permanent, similar and different, universal and local, like an echo of our own diversity and equality as persons.

Constructed with walls of white concrete and large sheets of colored glass, the MUSAC's single floor intends to be a space where art will be comfortable, where it can help to erase the frontiers between private and public, between leisure and work, between art and life.

Photographs: Luis Asin

Site plan

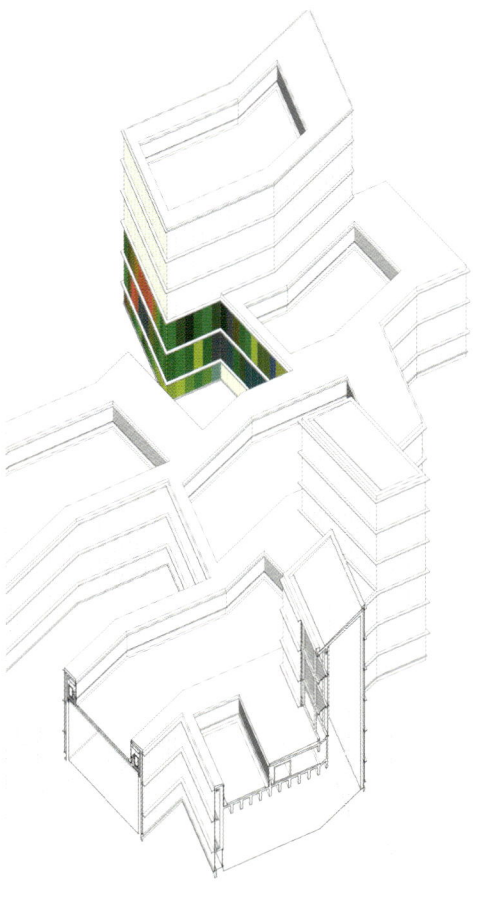

Ground floor plan

First floor plan

1. Hall
2. Staff
3. Office
4. Educational Whorkshop
5. Library
6. Toilets
7. Shop

8. Cafe
9. Multiuse room
10. Patio
11. Restoration whorkshop
12. Storage
13. Technical area
14. Restaurant

15. Load and storage
16. Loading area
17. Exhibition rooms
18. Exhibition patio
19. Public courtyard

159

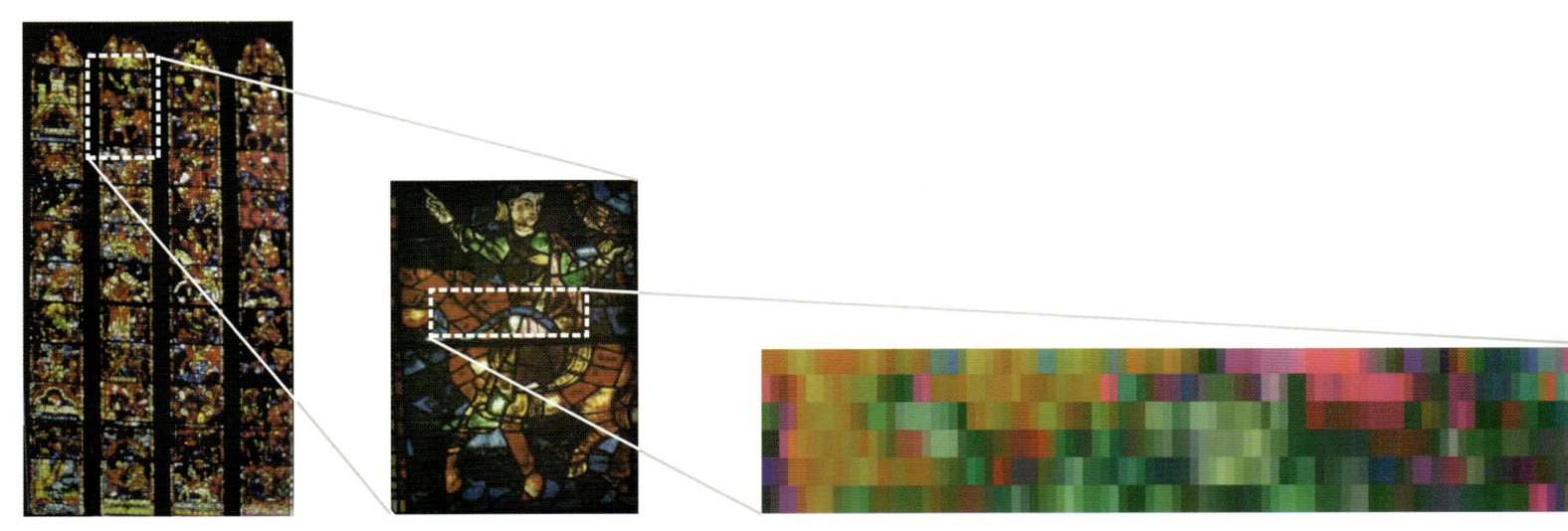

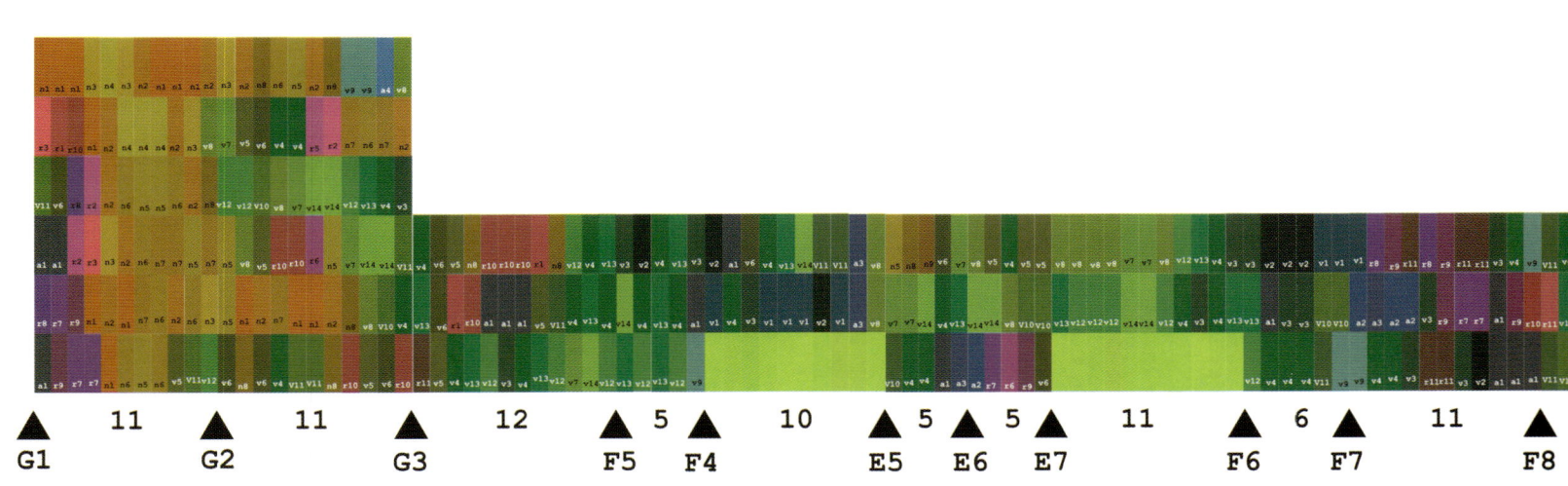

▲ 11 ▲ 11 ▲ 12 ▲ 5 ▲ 10 ▲ 5 ▲ 5 ▲ 11 ▲ 6 ▲ 11 ▲
G1　　　　G2　　　　G3　　　F5　F4　　　　E5　E6　E7　　　　F6　　F7　　　　F8

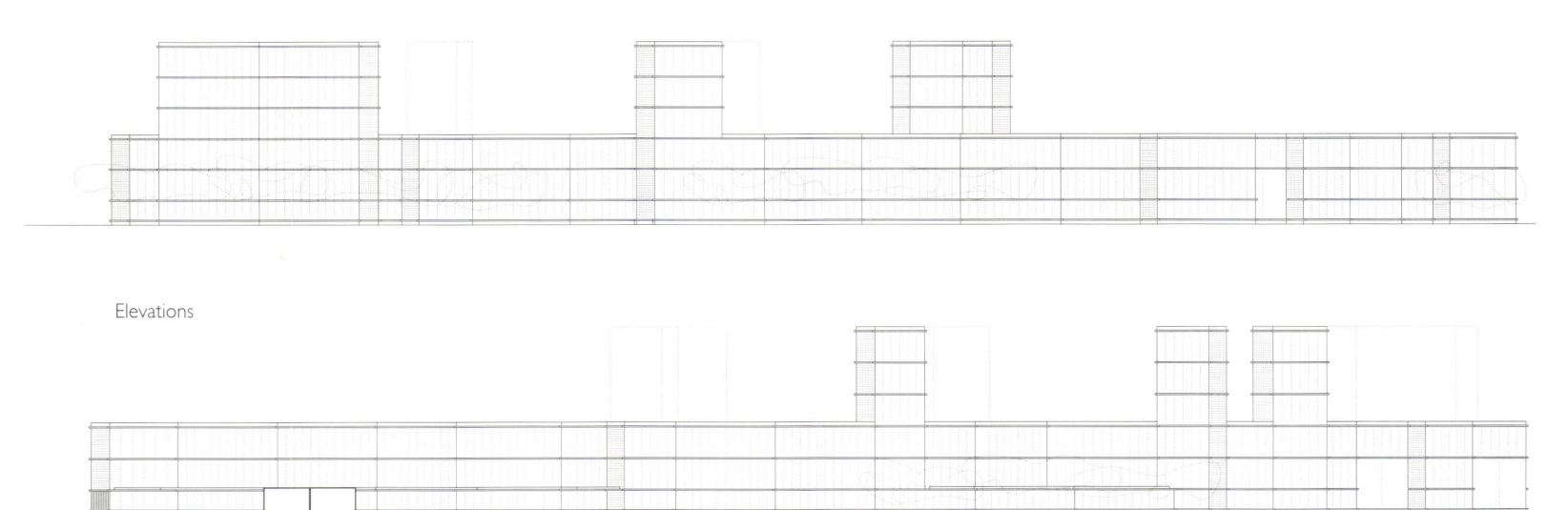

Elevations

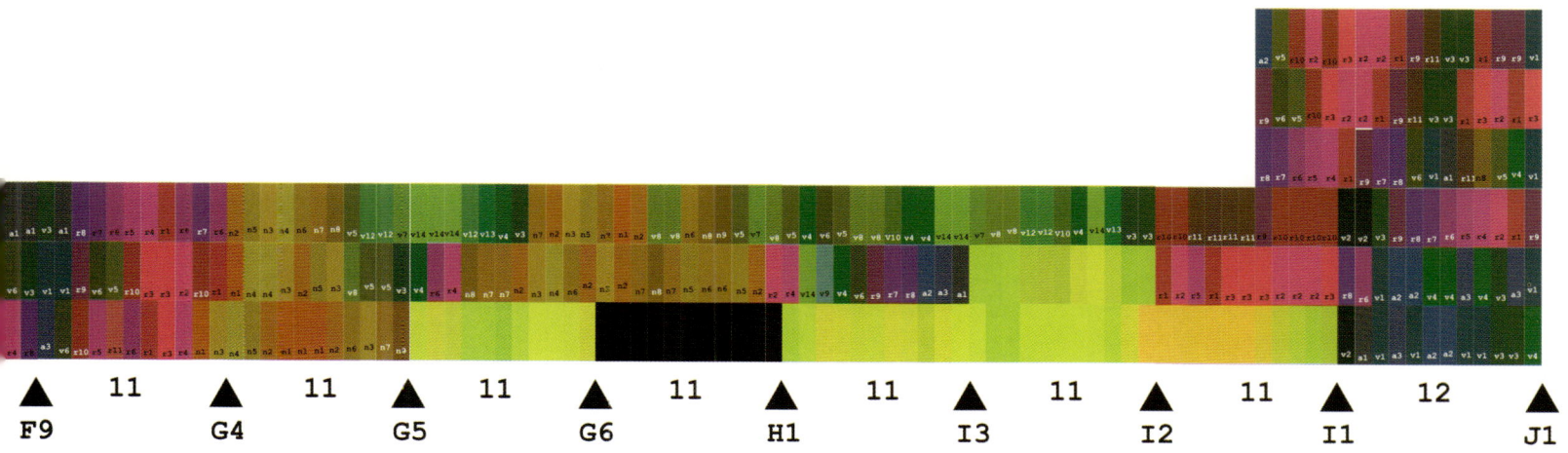

▲ 11 ▲ 11 ▲ 11 ▲ 11 ▲ 11 ▲ 11 ▲ 11 ▲ 11 ▲ 12 ▲
F9 G4 G5 G6 H1 I3 I2 I1 J1

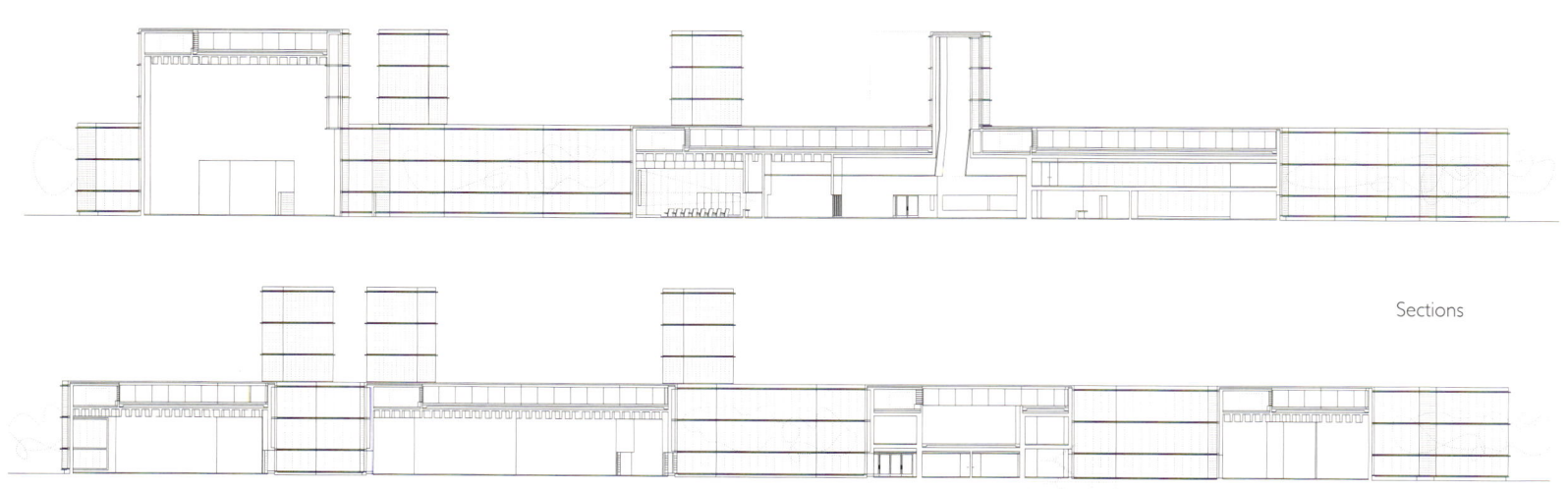

Sections

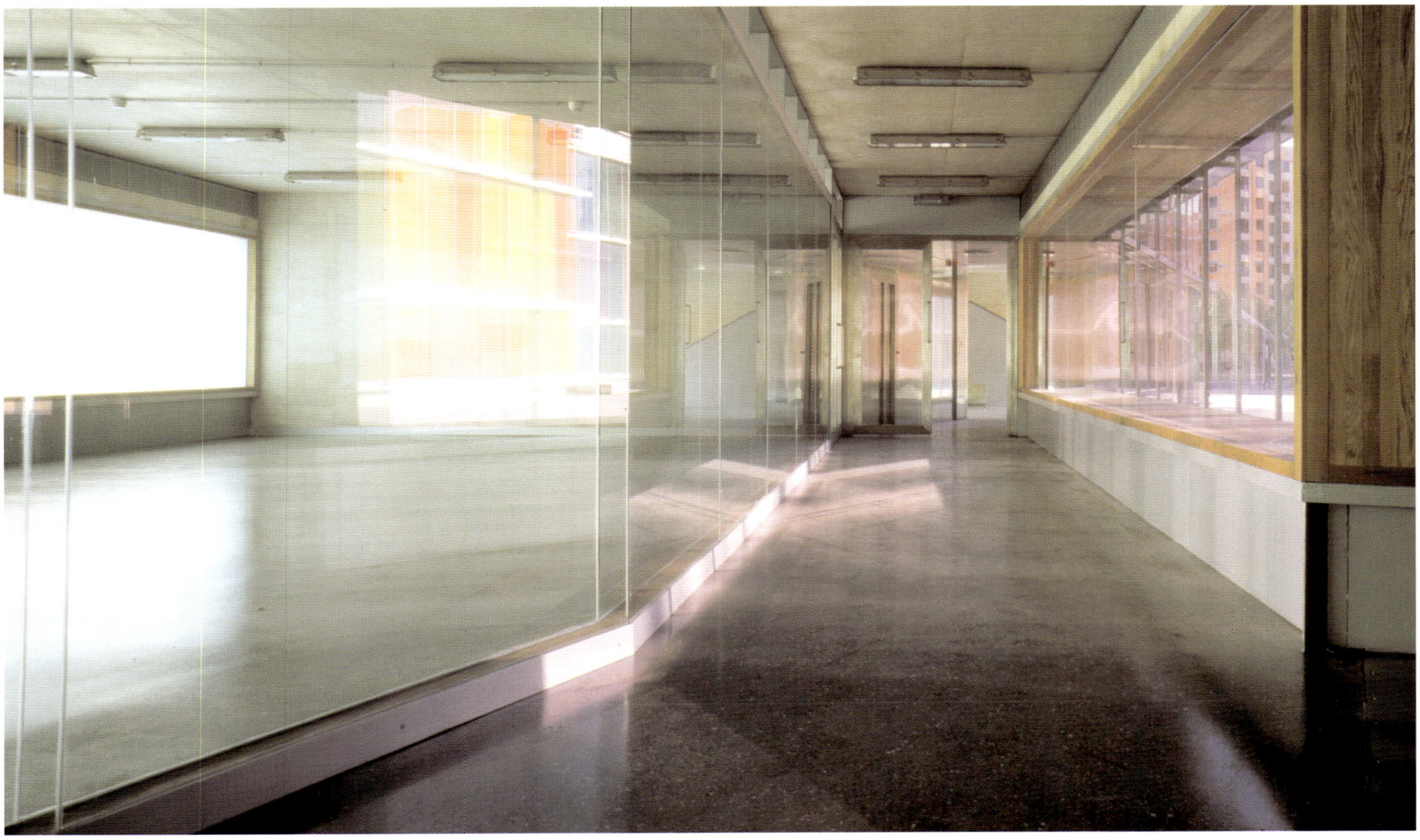

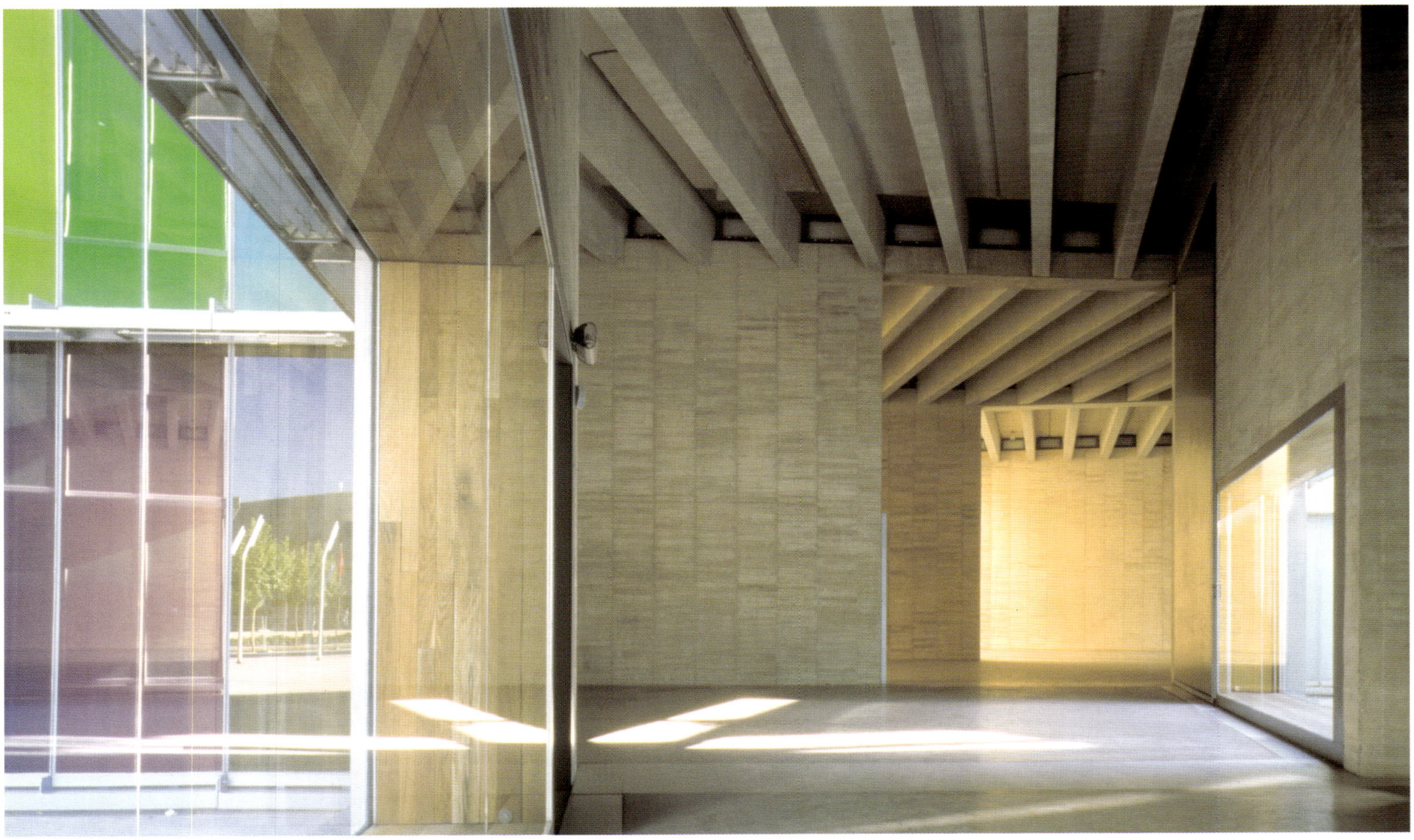

Santiago Calatrava
Príncipe Felipe Science Museum

València, Spain

The Príncipe Felipe Science Museum is located at the end of the immense complex of the City of Arts and Sciences, on the outskirts of Valencia. It is a complex full of stimulating buildings in which the architecture is forcefully expressive.

The building has five floors and a total area of 41,000 sqm. It is a large-scale building - 250 metres long by 54 high - and its structural system is a major feature accentuated by Calatrava's distinctive style, consisting of a long thin skeleton of great simplicity that brings a touch of elegance and sobriety to the City of Arts and Sciences. A double series of braces and flying buttresses set in this structure support the zig-zag roof that runs along the whole length of the museum. The building has an immense roof supported by a transparent glazed facade on the north side, whereas the south facade is opaque to block out the intense sunlight of the location.

One of the most important buildings of the museum is the Auditorium. It has a floor area of approximately 3,000 sqm and is a meeting point for the new technologies. The north foyer has similar proportions to the nave of a gothic cathedral, with ribs running along the total length of 180 metres. An entrance hall located on the upper level leads to a raised terrace, which is joined to the building as if it were supported by outstretched arms.

While the outside of the building features a large roof that seems to comb the sky of this spectacular architectural space, the internal structure features an impressive interplay of platforms suspended from a structural system formed by five large concrete "trees", whose branches support the roof of the building.

Photographs: Museu de les Ciències Archiv. / Javier Yaya Tur (CACSA)

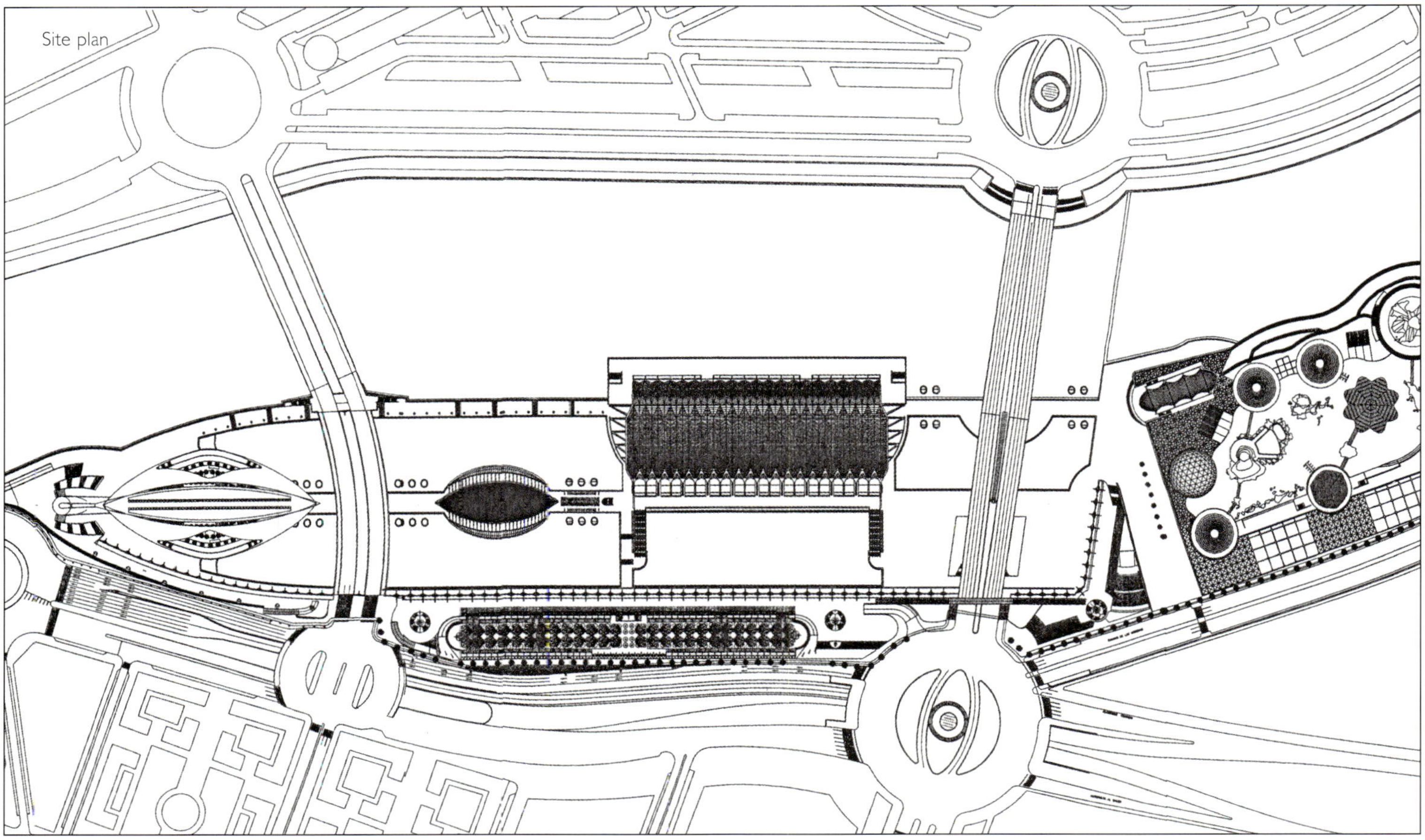
Site plan

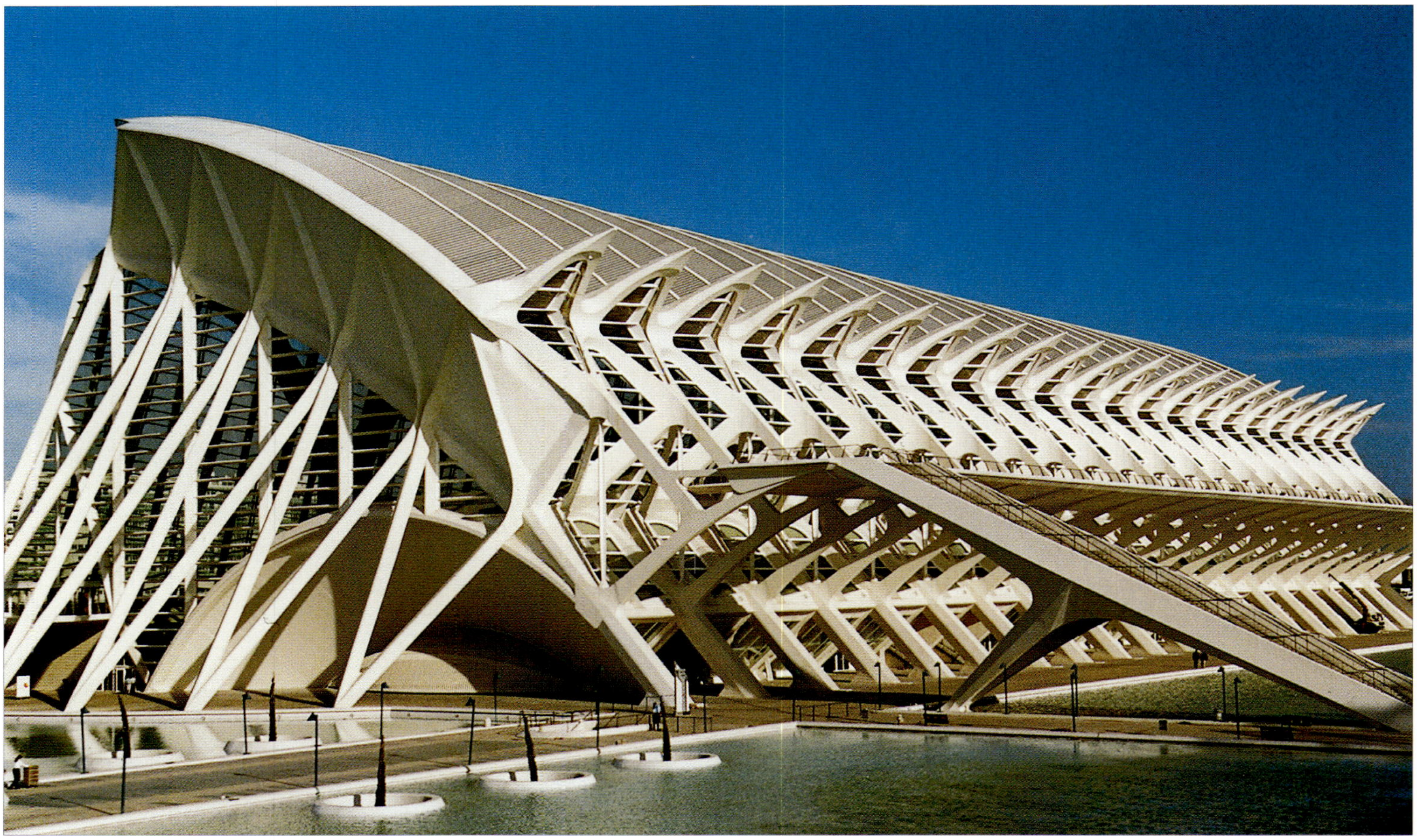

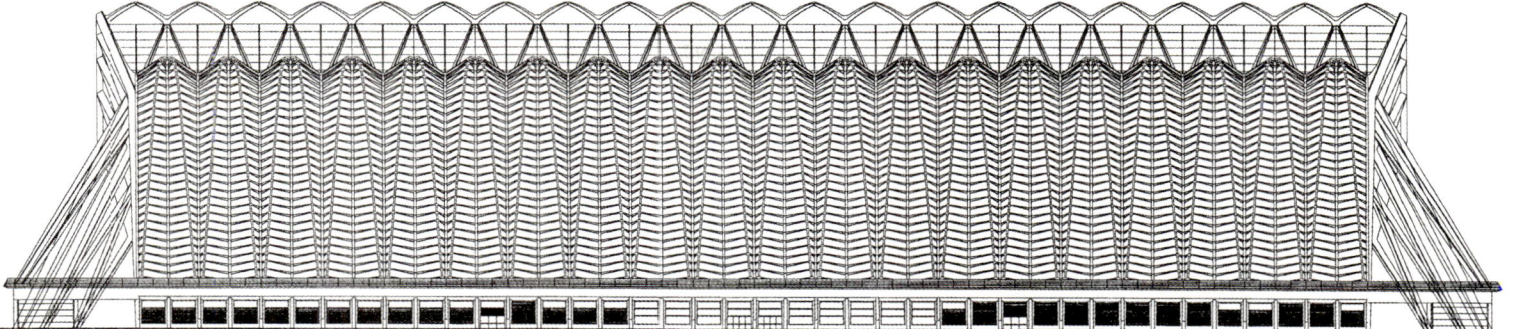

North elevation

South elevation

169

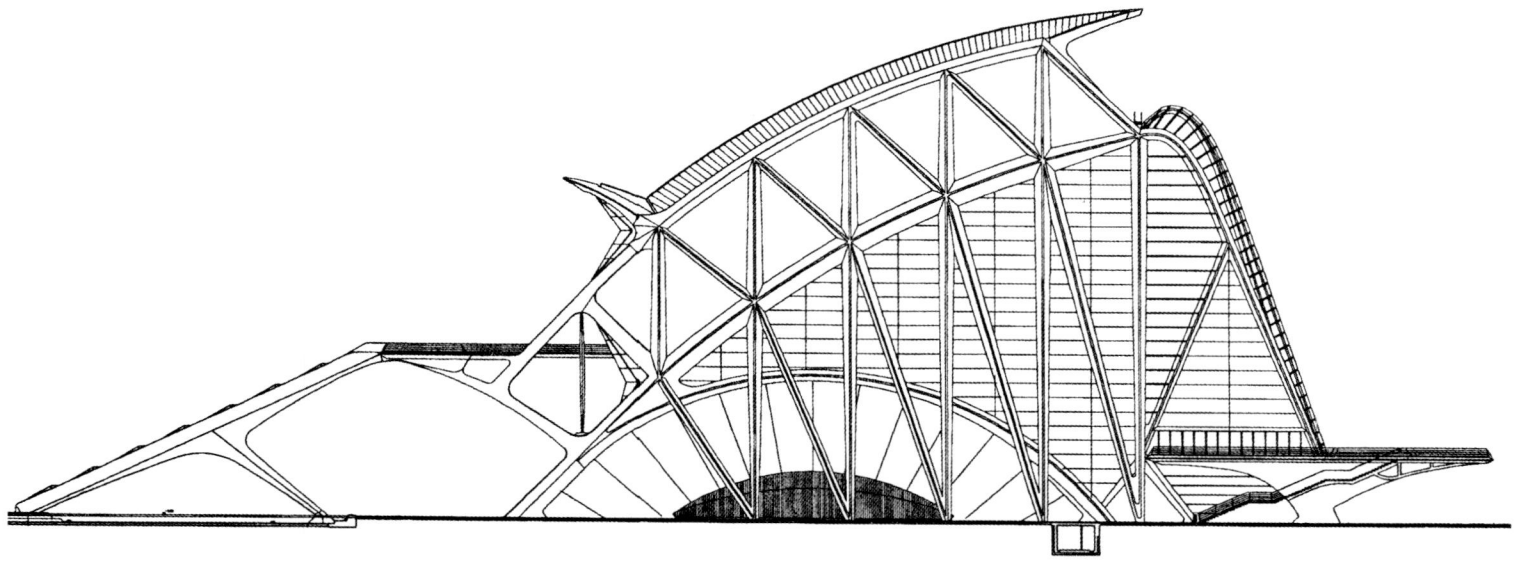

East elevation

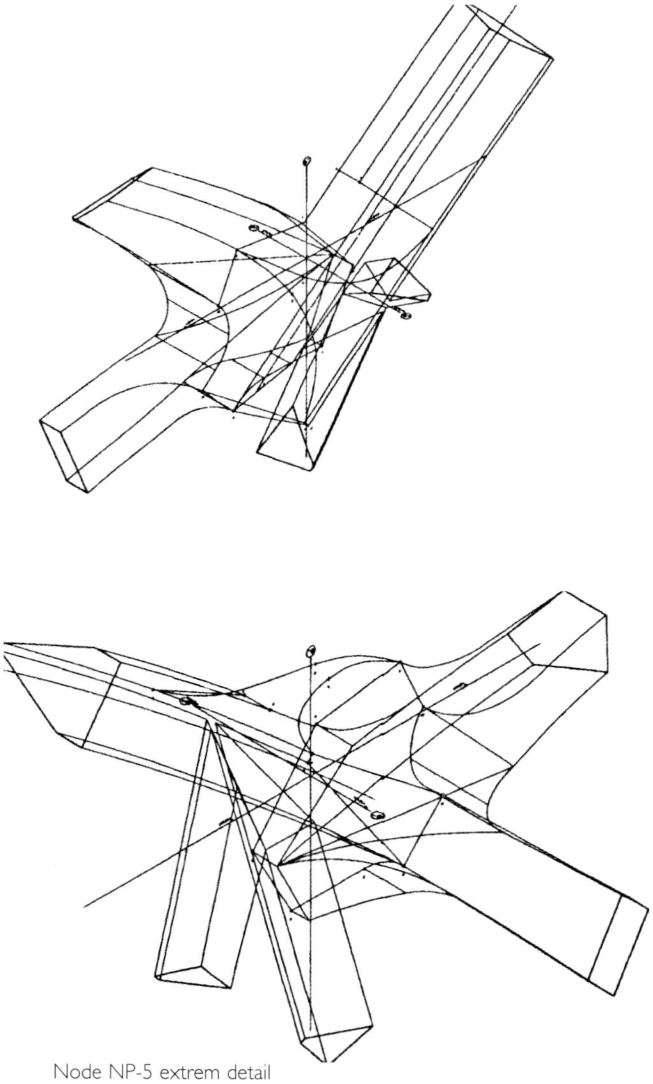

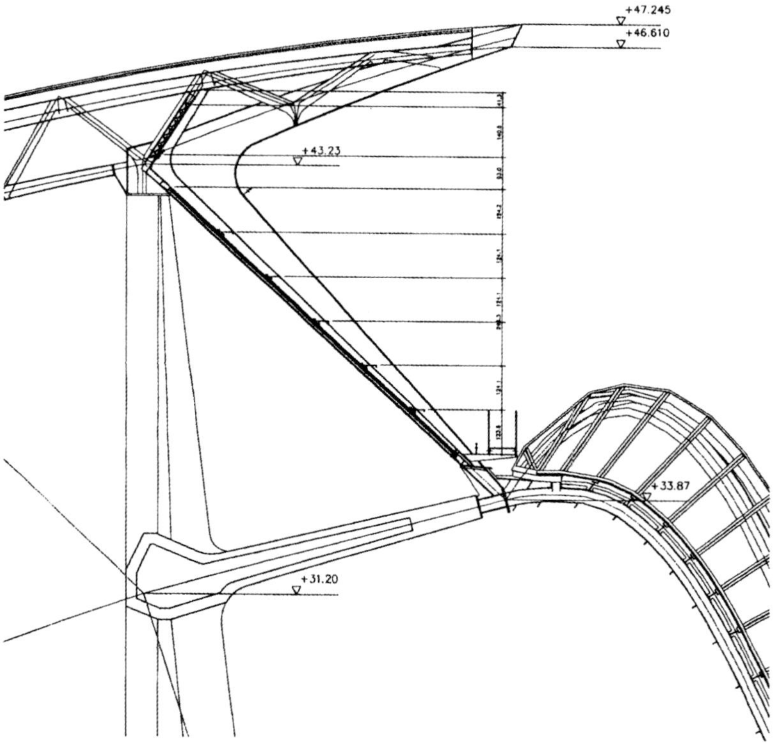

Node NP-5 extrem detail

South facade window detail

+47.245
+46.610
+43.23
+33.87
+31.20

The building appears as an immense roof supported by a transparent glazed facade on the north side, whereas the south facade is opaque to block out the intense sunlight of the location.

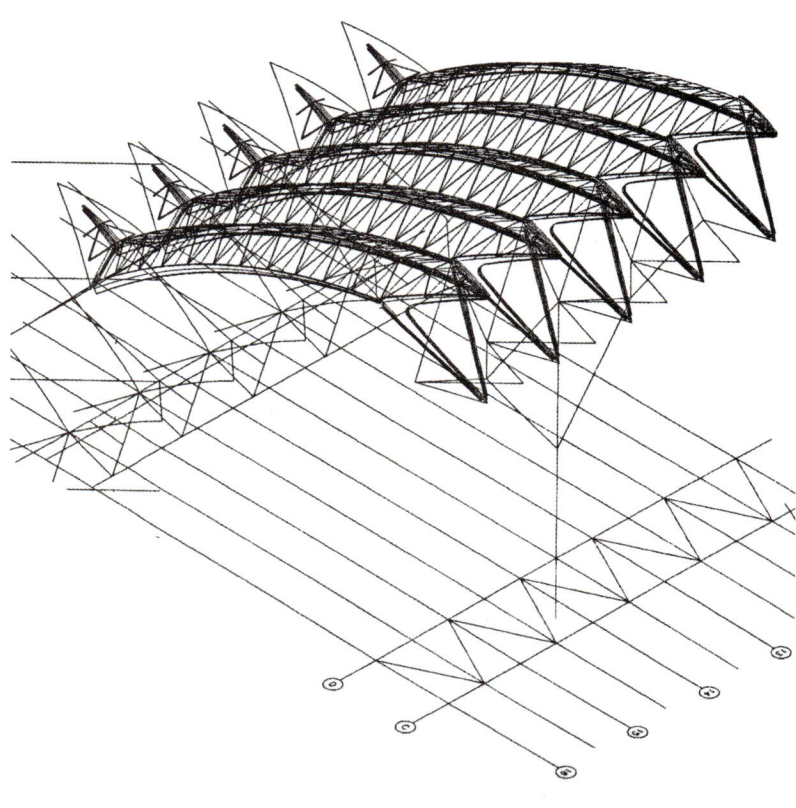

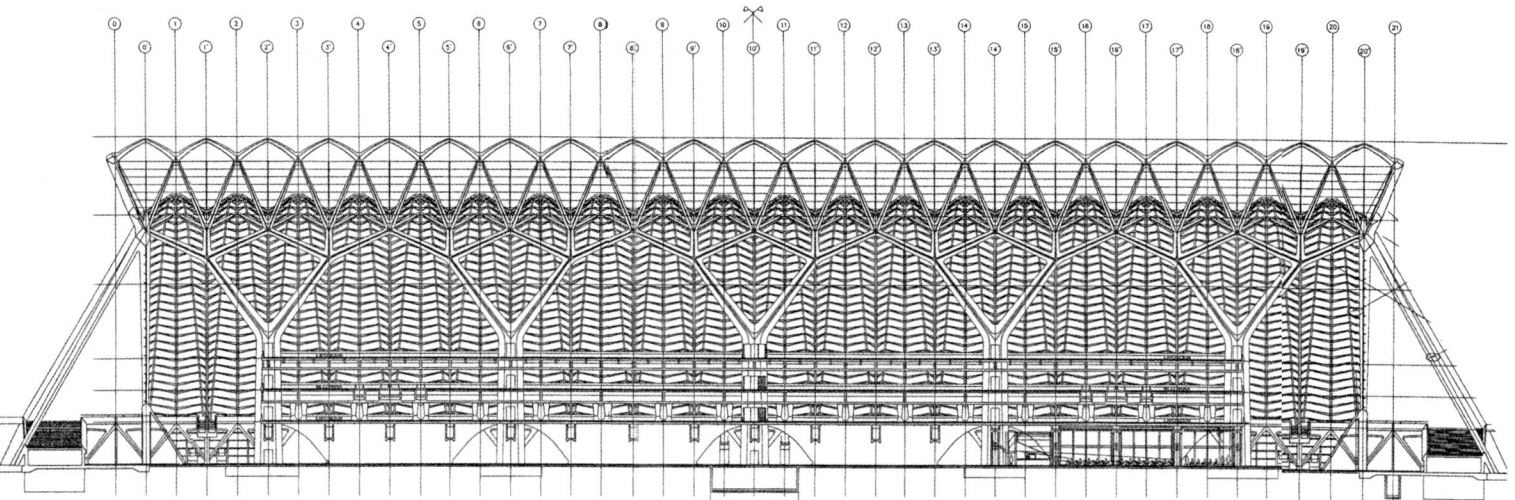

East-west. Longitudinal section

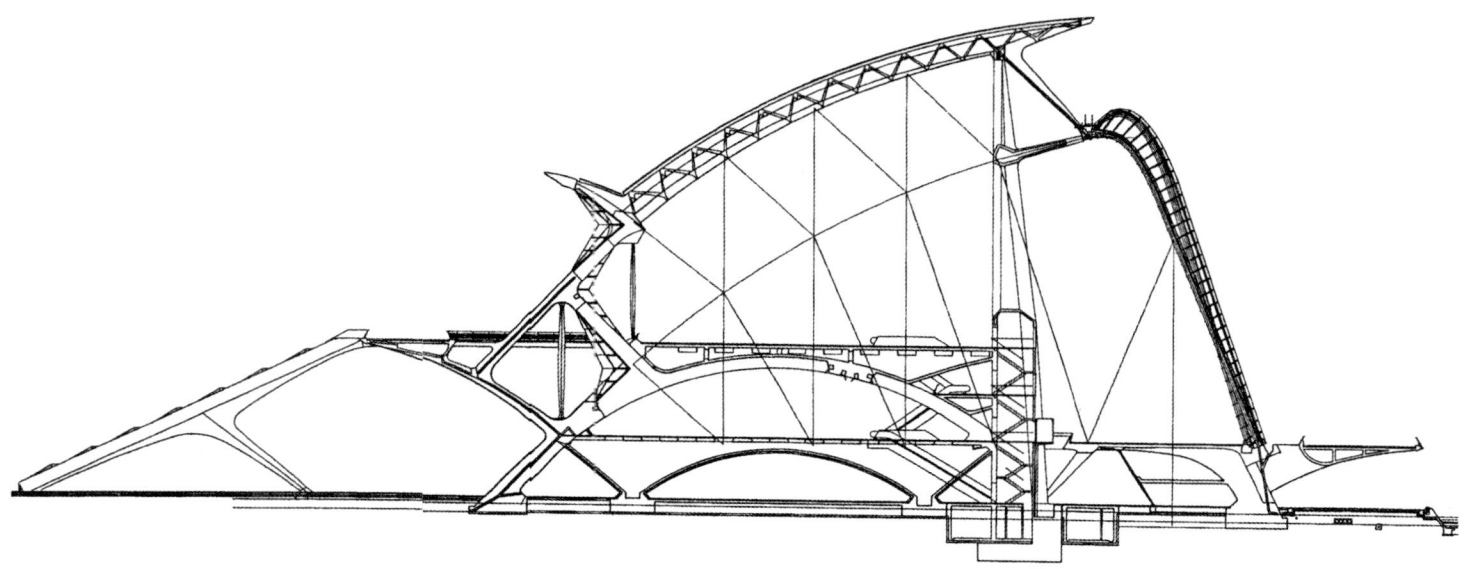

North-south. Cross-section by central tree

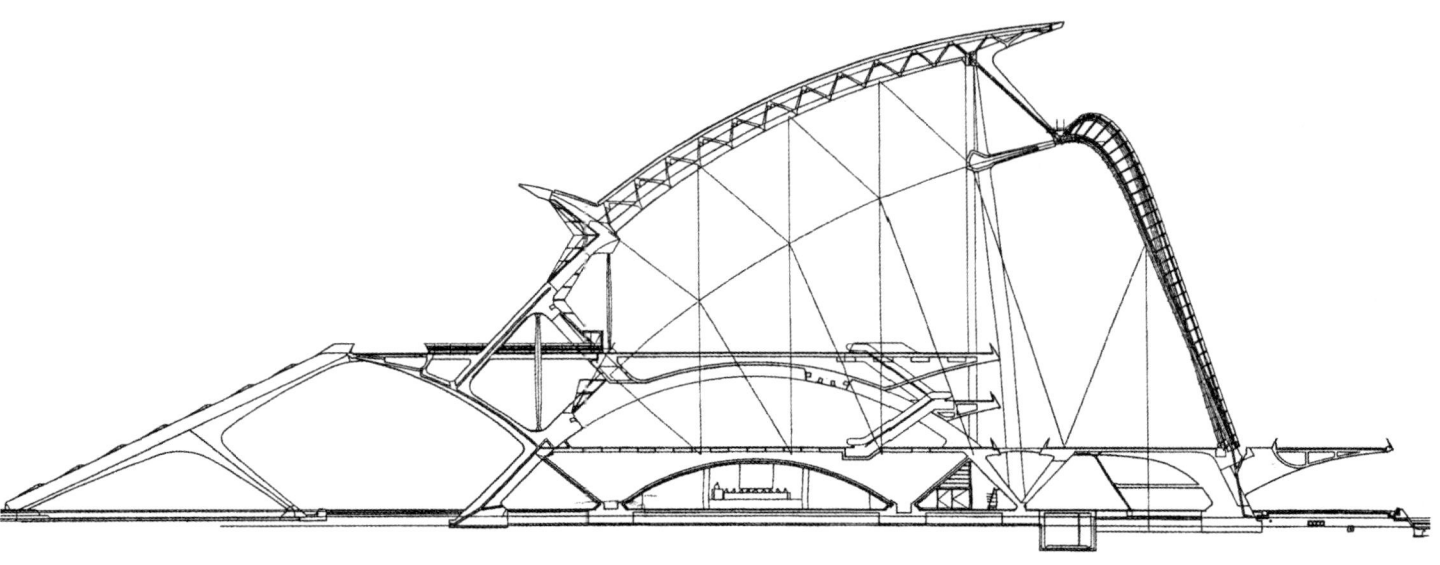

North-south. Cross-section

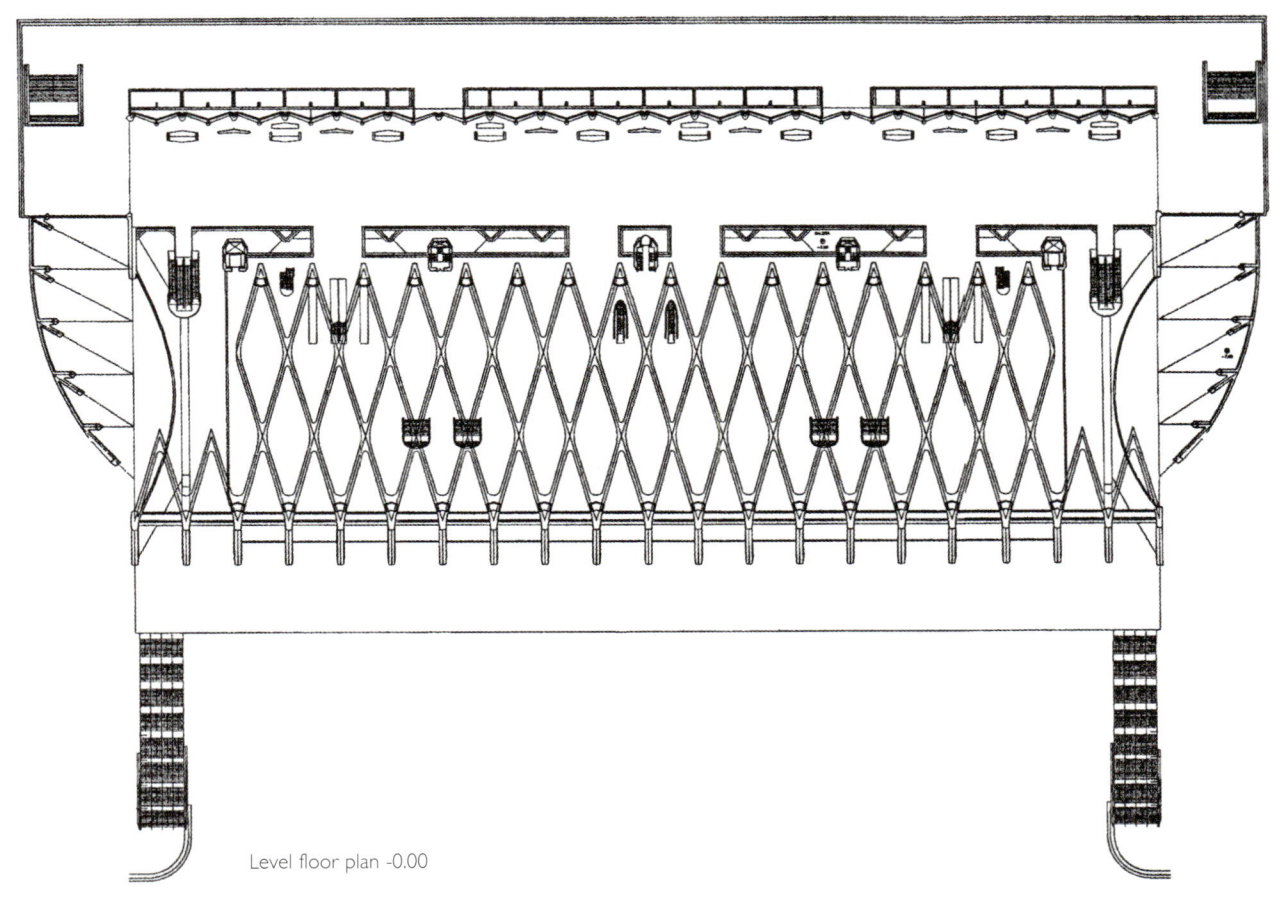

Level floor plan -0.00

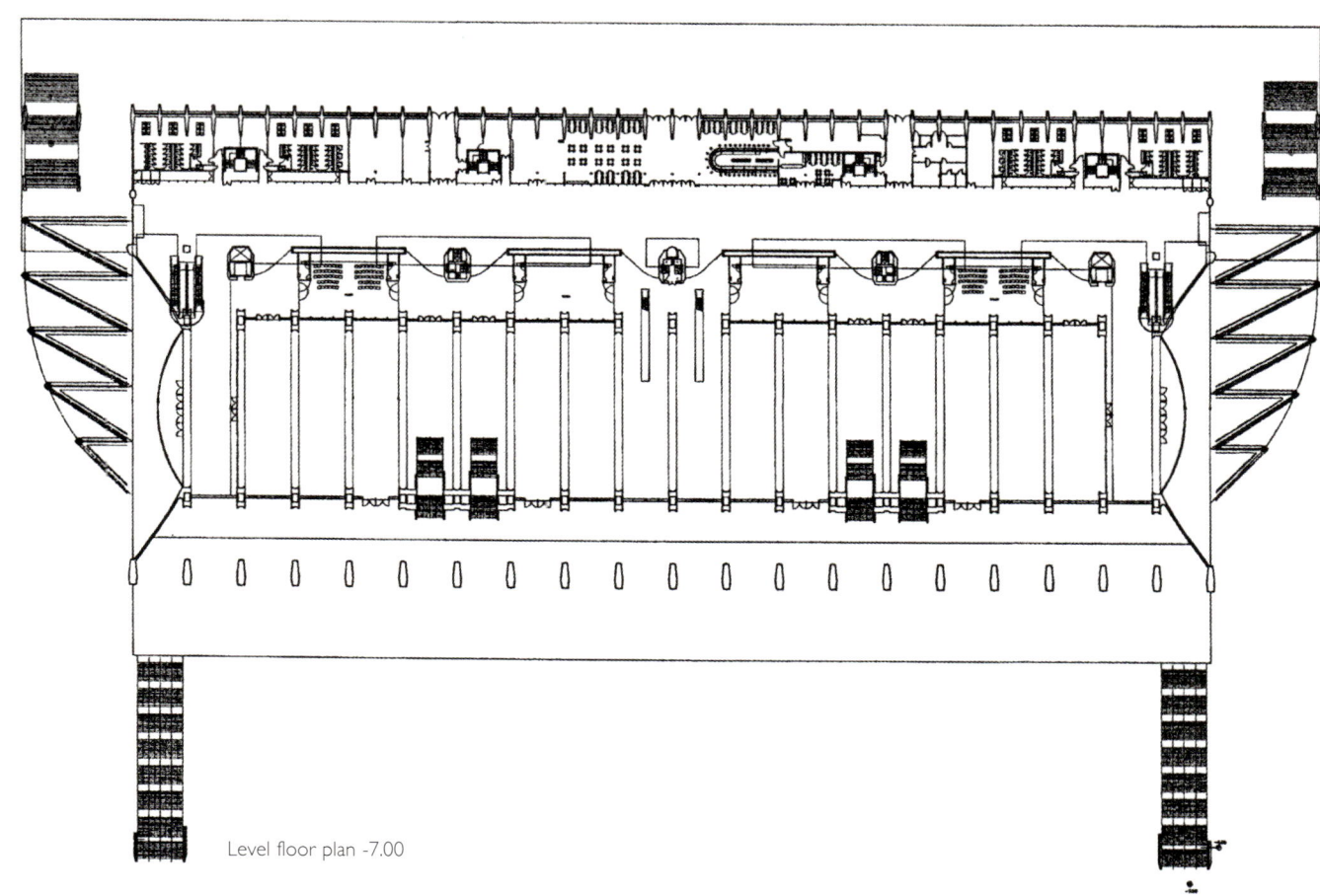

Level floor plan -7.00

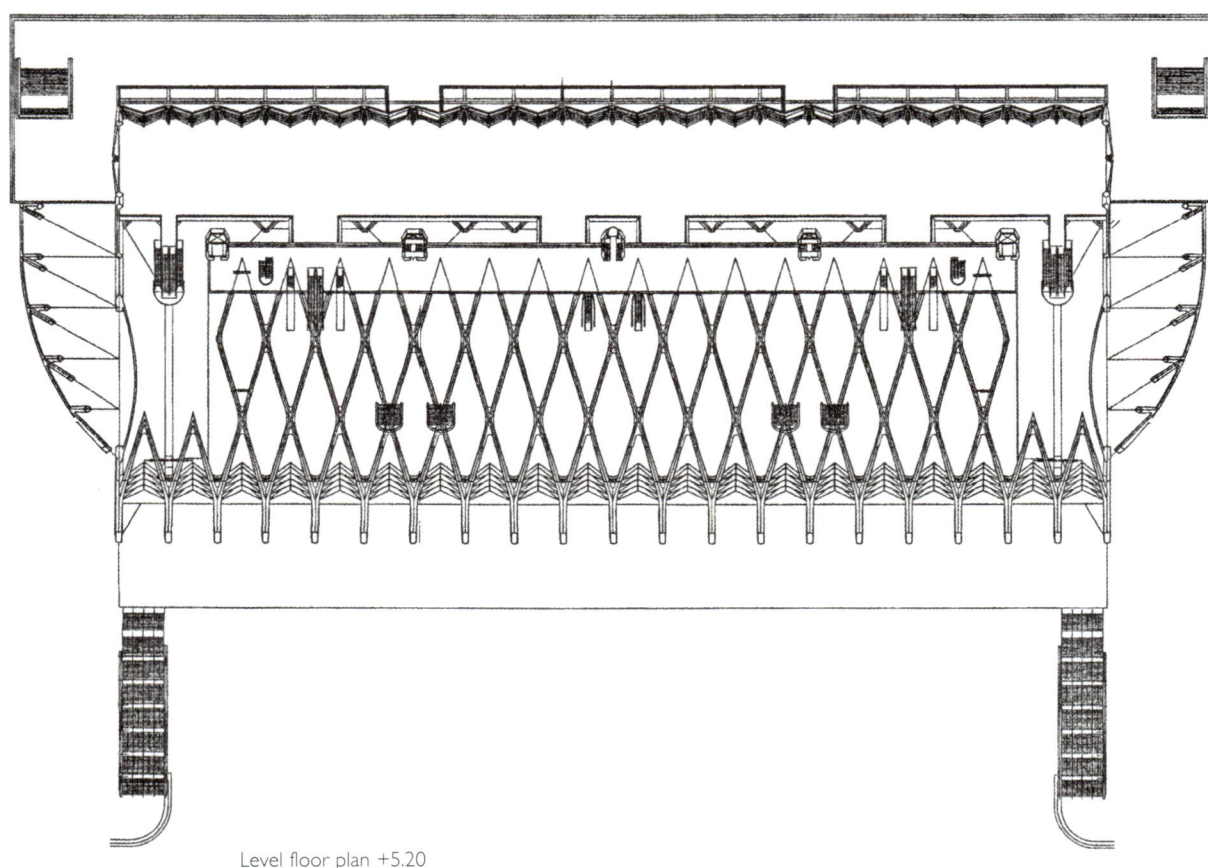
Level floor plan +5.20

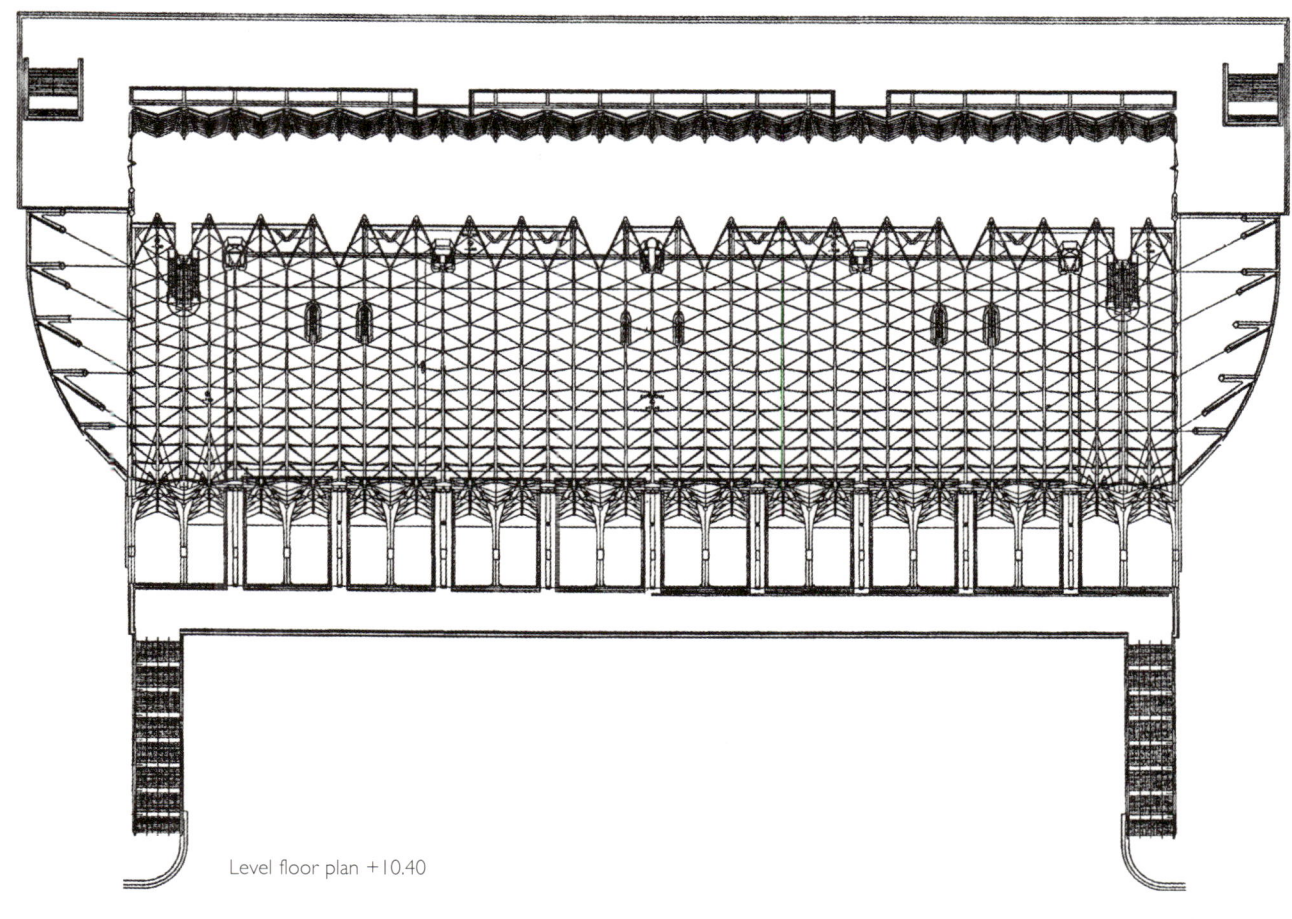

Level floor plan +10.40